Monolingual English Edition

The New Oxford Picture Dictionary

E. C. Parnwell

Illustrations by:
Ray Burns
Bob Giuliani
Laura Hartman
Pamela Johnson
Melodye Rosales
Raymond Skibinski
Joel Snyder

Oxford University Press

Oxford University Press

198 Madison Avenue
New York, NY 10016 USA

Great Clarendon Street
Oxford OX2 6DP England

Oxford New York
Athens Auckland Bangkok Bogotá Buenos Aires Calcutta
Cape Town Chennai Dar es Salaam Delhi Florence Hong Kong Istanbul
Karachi Kuala Lumpur Madrid Melbourne Mexico City Mumbai
Nairobi Paris São Paulo Singapore Taipei Tokyo Toronto Warsaw

and associated companies in
Berlin Ibadan

OXFORD is a trademark of Oxford University Press.

Library of Congress Cataloging-in-Publication Data

Parnwell, E. C.
    The new Oxford picture dictionary.
    Rev. ed. of: Oxford picture dictionary of American
English.
    1. Picture dictionaries, English. 2. English
language—United States—Dictionaries. 3. Americanisms—
Dictionaries. 4. English language—Text-books for
foreign speakers. I. Parnwell, E.C. Oxford picture
dictionary of American English. II. Title.
PE2835.P37   423'.1   87-23950
ISBN 0-19-434199-2 (softcover)
ISBN 0-19-434533-5 (hardcover)

Developmental Editor: Margot Gramer
Consulting Editor: Joan Saslow
Pronunciation editor: Clifford Hill, Columbia University
Associate Editor: Mary Lynne Nielsen
Editorial Assistant: Jeanne Rabenda
Art Director: Shireen Nathoo

The publishers would like to thank the following agents for their cooperation:

Carol Bancroft and Friends, representing Bob
Giuliani, Laura Hartman, and Melodye Rosales.
Publishers Graphics Inc., representing Ray Burns,
Pamela Johnson, and Joel Snyder.

Cover illustration by Laura Hartman.

Softcover Printing (last digit): 29 28 27 26 25 24
Hardcover Printing (last digit): 10 9 8 7 6 5

Printed in Hong Kong

The New Oxford Picture Dictionary contextually illustrates over 2,400 words. The book is a unique language learning tool for students of English. It provides students with a glance at American lifestyle, as well as a compendium of useful vocabulary.

The *Dictionary* is organized thematically, beginning with topics that are most useful for the "survival" needs of students in an English-speaking country. The topics move on to those of a more general nature, including those that might be used in content area classes in schools in the United States. However, pages may be used at random, depending on the students' particular needs. The book need not be taught in order.

The words depicted are those most useful for students needing basic English skills. The most common name of any given item was used for simplicity. Any regionalisms or variations will be found in the *Teacher's Guide* for that particular page.

The New Oxford Picture Dictionary contextualizes vocabulary whenever possible, thus making the language learner's task a bit easier. Verbs have been included on separate pages, but within a topic area where they are most likely to occur. However, this does not imply that these verbs only appear within these contexts.

For obvious reasons, the number of words per page has been limited. In addition, attempts have been made to place the numbers on the art consecutively, either from left to right, or, on many contextualized pages, in a circular, clockwise order.

A complete index with pronunciation guide has been included in the Appendix. For further ideas on using *The New Oxford Picture Dictionary*, see the *Listening and Speaking Activity Book*, the *Teacher's Guide*, and the two workbooks: *Beginner's* and *Intermediate* levels.

Also available in the program are a complete set of *Cassettes*, offering a reading of all the words in the *Dictionary*; *Vocabulary Playing Cards*, featuring 40 words and the corresponding pictures on 80 cards with ideas for many games; sets of *Wall Charts*, available in one complete package, or in three smaller packages; and *Overhead Transparencies*, featuring color transparencies of all the *Dictionary* pages. The *NOPD CD-ROM* offers the complete *Dictionary* in an interactive multimedia format and includes exercises and activities.

iv Contents

People and Relationships	*Page*	2
The Family		3
The Human Body		4–5
Vegetables		6–7
Fruits		8–9
Meat, Poultry, and Seafood		10–11
Containers, Quantities, and Money		12–13
The Supermarket		14–15
Family Restaurant and Cocktail Lounge		16
Restaurant Verbs		17
Common Prepared Foods		18
Outdoor Clothes		19
Everyday Clothes		20–21
Underwear and Sleepwear		22
Jewelry and Cosmetics		23
Describing Clothes		24
Describing the Weather		25
Seasonal Verbs		26
Houses		27
The Living Room		28
The Dining Room		29
The Kitchen		30
Kitchen Verbs		31
The Bedroom		32
The Baby's Room		33
The Bathroom		34
The Utility Room		35
A Workshop		36–37
Housework and Repair Verbs		38
Medical and Dental Care		39
Ailments and Injuries		40
Treatments and Remedies		41
Firefighting and Rescue		42
Crime and Punishment		43
The City		44–45
The U.S. Postal System		46
The Public Library		47
The Armed Forces		48
Trucks		49
Cars		50–51
Bikes		52
Highway Travel		53
Public Transportation		54–55

	Page	
Air Travel		56
Aircraft		57
In Port		58
Pleasure Boating		59
Plants and Trees		60–61
Simple Animals		62
Insects		63
Birds		64
Fish and Reptiles		65
Mammals I		66–67
Mammals II		68–69
Map of the World		70–71
The United States of America		72–73
The Universe		74
The Space Program		75
A Classroom		76
School Verbs		77
A Science Lab		78
Math		79
Energy		80
Farming and Ranching		81
Construction		82
An Office		83
Occupations I: Main Street USA		84
Occupations II		85
Occupations III		86
Neighborhood Parks		87
Outdoor Activities		88–89
At the Beach		90–91
Team Sports		92
Ballfields		93
Individual Sports		94
Fields and Courses		95
Sports Verbs		96–97
Musical Instruments		98
Music, Dance, and Theater		99
Electronics and Photography		100
Handicrafts		101
Prepositions of Description		102
Prepositions of Motion		103
Appendix		104
Index		105

1. woman
2. man
3. husband
4. wife
5. baby
6. parents
7. children
8. boy
9. girl
10. grandparents
11. granddaughter
12. grandson

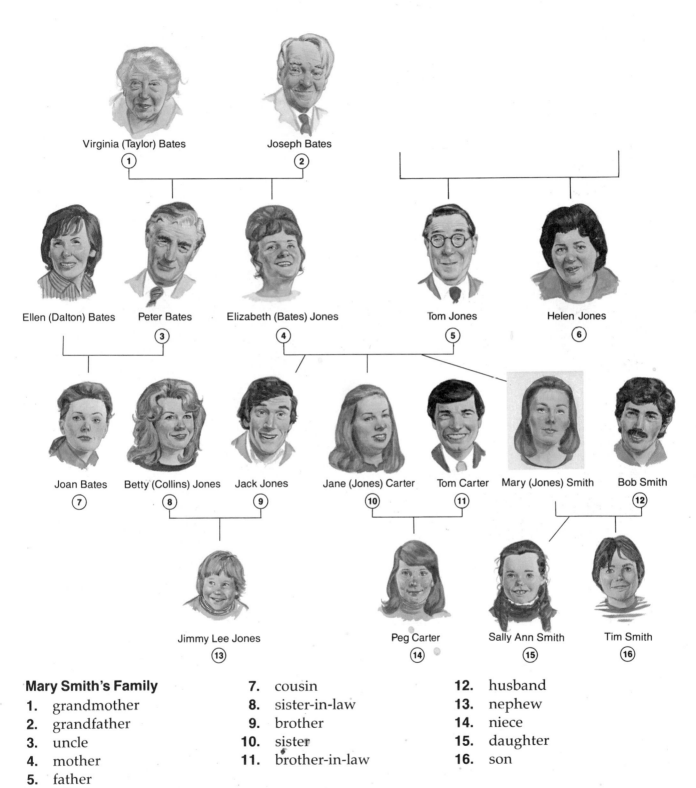

Virginia (Taylor) Bates ①   Joseph Bates ②

Ellen (Dalton) Bates   Peter Bates ③   Elizabeth (Bates) Jones ④   Tom Jones ⑤   Helen Jones ⑥

Joan Bates ⑦   Betty (Collins) Jones ⑧   Jack Jones ⑨   Jane (Jones) Carter ⑩   Tom Carter ⑪   Mary (Jones) Smith   Bob Smith ⑫

Jimmy Lee Jones ⑬   Peg Carter ⑭   Sally Ann Smith ⑮   Tim Smith ⑯

Mary Smith's Family

1. grandmother
2. grandfather
3. uncle
4. mother
5. father
6. aunt
7. cousin
8. sister-in-law
9. brother
10. sister
11. brother-in-law
12. husband
13. nephew
14. niece
15. daughter
16. son

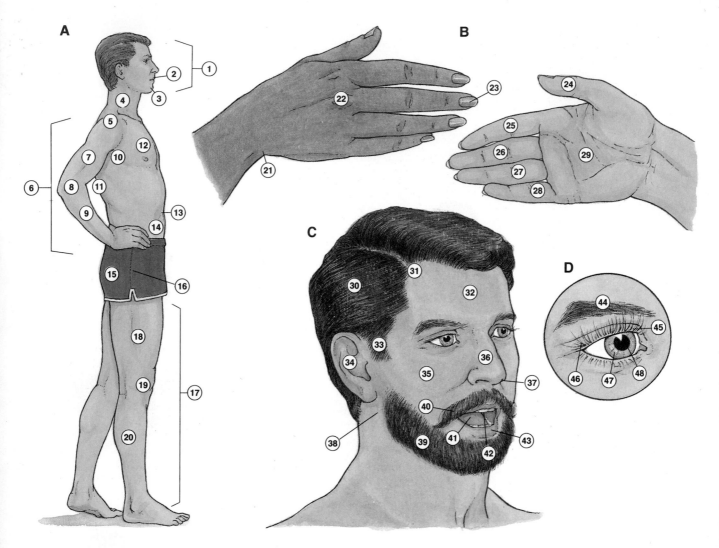

A.   The Body
1. face
2. mouth
3. chin
4. neck
5. shoulder
6. arm
7. upper arm
8. elbow
9. forearm
10. armpit
11. back
12. chest
13. waist
14. abdomen
15. buttocks
16. hip
17. leg
18. thigh
19. knee
20. calf

B.   The Hand
21. wrist
22. knuckle
23. fingernail
24. thumb
25. (index) finger
26. middle finger
27. ring finger
28. little finger
29. palm

C.   The Head
30. hair
31. part
32. forehead
33. sideburn
34. ear
35. cheek
36. nose
37. nostril
38. jaw
39. beard
40. mustache
41. tongue
42. tooth
43. lip

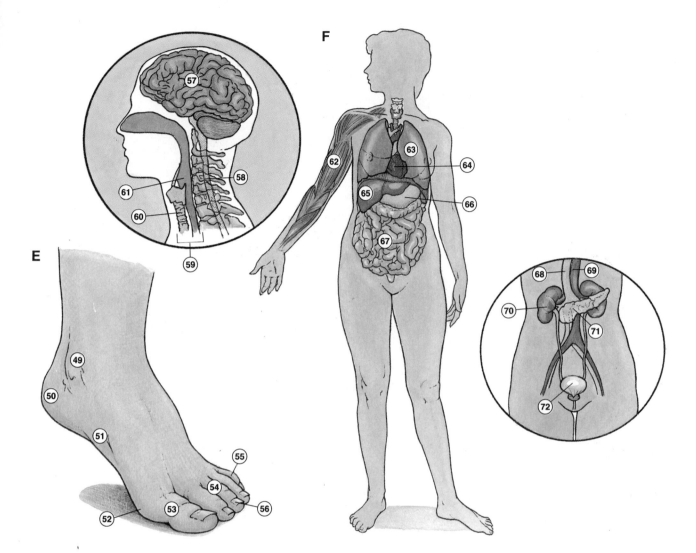

D. The Eye
44. eyebrow
45. eyelid
46. eyelashes
47. iris
48. pupil

E. The Foot
49. ankle
50. heel
51. instep
52. ball
53. big toe
54. toe
55. little toe
56. toenail

F. The Internal Organs
57. brain
58. spinal cord
59. throat
60. windpipe
61. esophagus
62. muscle
63. lung
64. heart
65. liver
66. stomach
67. intestines
68. vein
69. artery
70. kidney
71. pancreas
72. bladder

1. (head of) cauliflower
2. broccoli
3. cabbage
4. brussels sprouts
5. watercress
6. lettuce
7. escarole
8. spinach
9. herb(s)
10. celery
11. artichoke
12. (ear of) corn
   a. cob
13. kidney bean(s)
14. black bean(s)
15. string bean(s)
16. lima bean(s)
17. pea(s)
   a. pod
18. asparagus

19. tomato(es)	**24.** yam	**29.** radish(es)
20. cucumber(s)	**25.** garlic	**30.** mushroom(s)
21. eggplant	**a.** clove	**31.** onion(s)
22. pepper(s)	**26.** pumpkin	**32.** carrot(s)
23. potato(es)	**27.** zucchini	**33.** beet(s)
	28. acorn squash	**34.** turnip

1. (a bunch of) grapes
2. apple
   a. stem
   b. core
3. coconut
4. pineapple
5. mango
6. papaya

Citrus Fruits

7. grapefruit
8. orange
   a. section
   b. rind
   c. seed
9. lemon
10. lime

Berries

11. gooseberries
12. blackberries
13. cranberries
14. blueberries
15. strawberry
16. raspberries

17. nectarine
18. pear

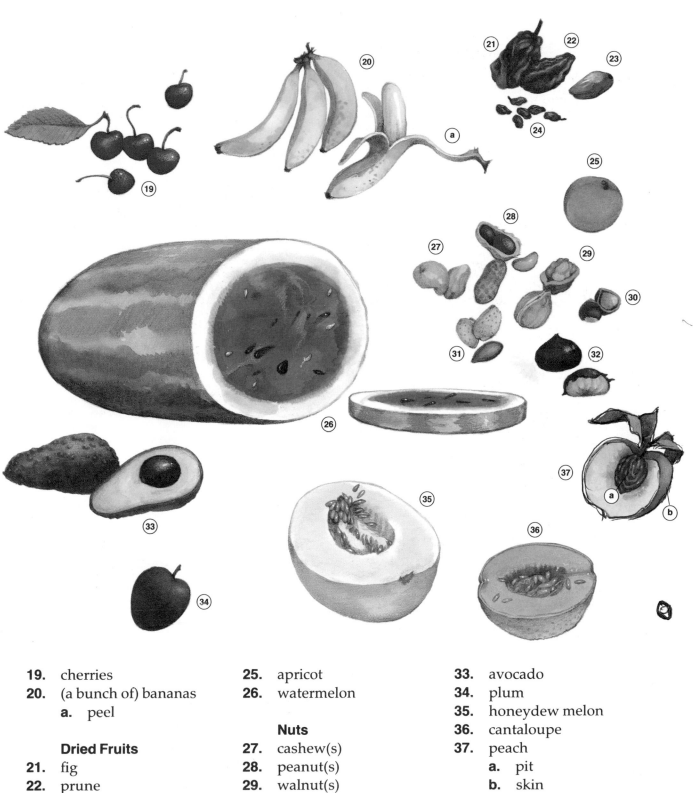

19. cherries
20. (a bunch of) bananas
    a. peel

Dried Fruits
21. fig
22. prune
23. date
24. raisin(s)

25. apricot
26. watermelon

Nuts
27. cashew(s)
28. peanut(s)
29. walnut(s)
30. hazelnut(s)
31. almond(s)
32. chestnut(s)

33. avocado
34. plum
35. honeydew melon
36. cantaloupe
37. peach
    a. pit
    b. skin

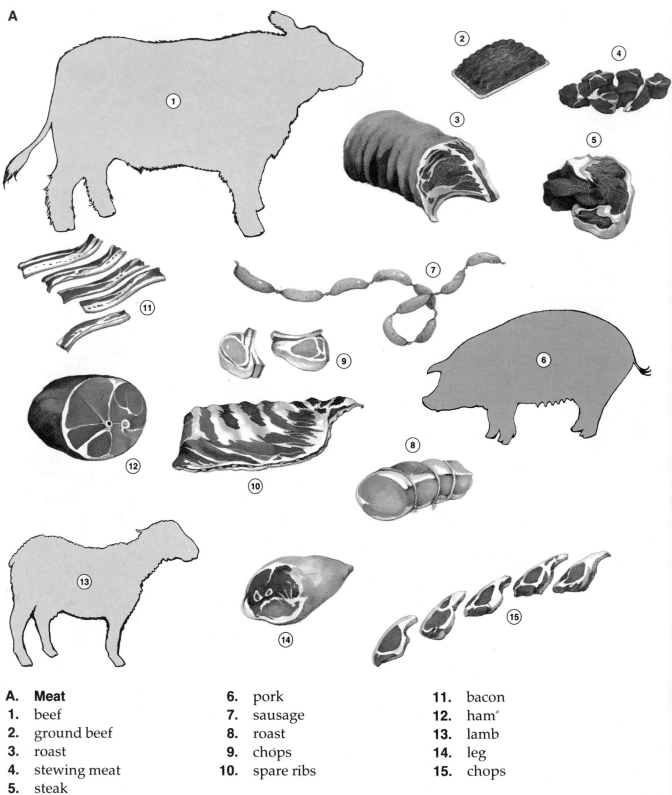

A. **Meat**
1. beef
2. ground beef
3. roast
4. stewing meat
5. steak
6. pork
7. sausage
8. roast
9. chops
10. spare ribs
11. bacon
12. ham
13. lamb
14. leg
15. chops

B

C

D

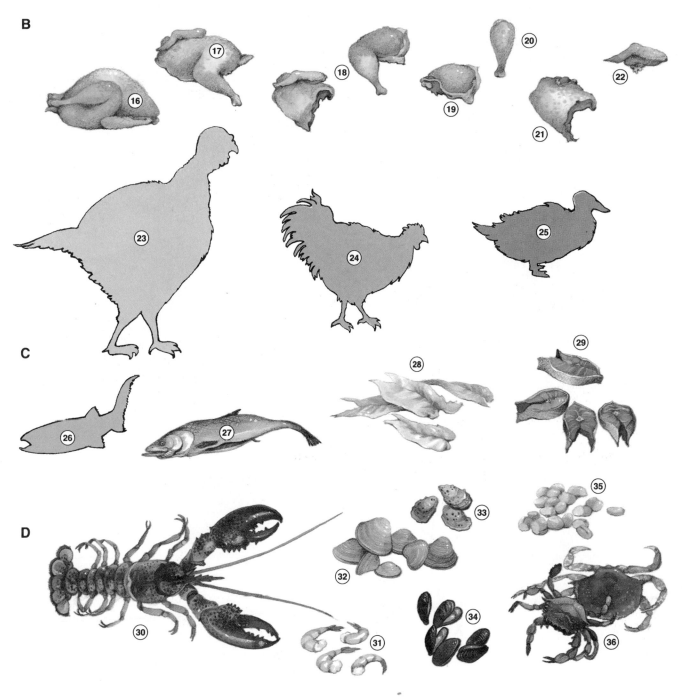

B.	**Poultry**	24.	chicken	D.	**Shellfish**
16.	whole (chicken)	25.	duck	30.	lobster
17.	split			31.	shrimp
18.	quarter	C.	**Seafood**	32.	clam(s)
19.	thigh	26.	fish	33.	oyster(s)
20.	leg	27.	whole	34.	mussel(s)
21.	breast	28.	filet	35.	scallop(s)
22.	wing	29.	steak	36.	crab(s)
23.	turkey				

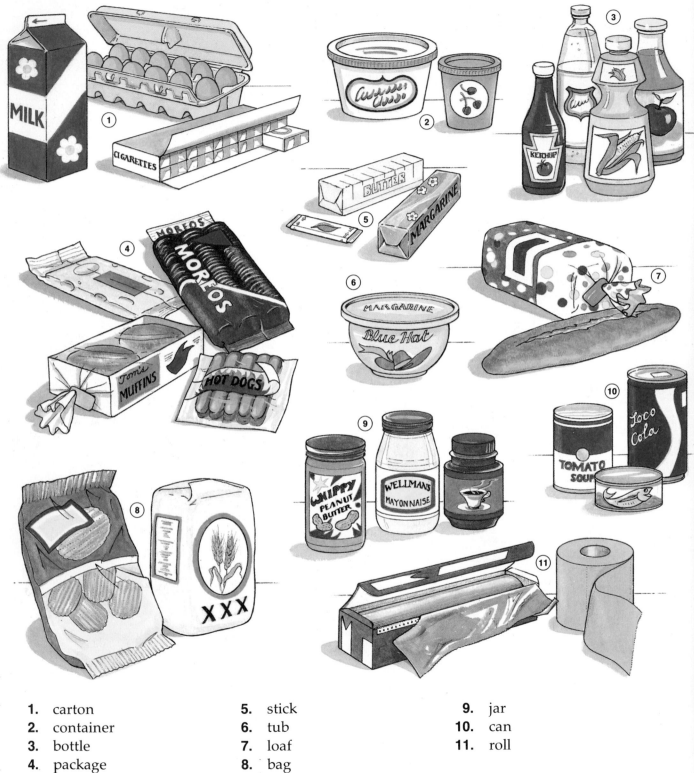

1. carton
2. container
3. bottle
4. package
5. stick
6. tub
7. loaf
8. bag
9. jar
10. can
11. roll

12. box	**19.** cup	**Money**
13. six-pack	**20.** glass	**25.** dollar bills
14. pump	**21.** slice	**26.** coins
15. tube	**22.** piece	**27.** penny
16. pack	**23.** bowl	**28.** nickel
17. book	**24.** spray can	**29.** dime
18. bar		**30.** quarter

1. deli counter	6. shelf	11. baked goods
2. frozen foods	7. scale	12. bread
3. freezer	8. shopping basket	13. canned goods
4. dairy products	9. produce	14. beverages
5. milk	10. aisle	

FISH   MEAT   POULTRY

EXPRESS LANE 10 ITEMS OR LESS

15. household items	**20.** receipt	**24.** groceries
16. bin	**21.** cash register	**25.** bag
17. customer	**22.** cashier	**26.** checkout counter
18. snacks	**23.** conveyor belt	**27.** check
19. shopping cart		

A. Family Restaurant

1. cook
2. waitress
3. busboy
4. ketchup
5. waiter
6. apron
7. menu
8. high chair
9. booth
10. straw
11. soft drink
12. jukebox
13. sugar (packet)
14. check
15. tea
16. sandwich

B. Cocktail Lounge

17. corkscrew
18. cork
19. wine
20. tap
21. bartender
22. liquor (bottle)
23. beer
24. bar
25. bar stool
26. pipe
27. coaster
28. (book of) matches
29. ashtray
30. lighter
31. cigarette
32. cocktail waitress
33. tray

1. eat
2. drink
3. serve
4. cook
5. order
6. clear
7. pay
8. set (the table)
9. give
10. take
11. spread
12. hold
13. light
14. burn

1. mustard
2. hot dog
3. baked beans
4. potato chips
5. pancakes
6. syrup
7. bun
8. pickle
9. hamburger
10. spaghetti
11. meatballs
12. salad dressing

13. tossed salad
14. beef stew
15. pork chops
16. mixed vegetables
17. mashed potatoes
18. butter
19. roll
20. baked potato
21. steak
22. cookie
23. sundae
24. taco

25. egg roll
26. strawberry shortcake
27. biscuit
28. french fries
29. fried chicken
30. pizza
31. jelly
32. (sunnyside-up) egg
33. bacon
34. toast
35. coffee
36. ice cream cone

1. gloves	**10.** earmuffs	**18.** hat
2. cap	**11.** mittens	**19.** scarf
3. flannel shirt	**12.** down vest	**20.** overcoat
4. backpack	**13.** (turtleneck) sweater	**21.** boots
5. windbreaker	**14.** tights	**22.** beret
6. (blue) jeans	**15.** ice skates	**23.** (V-neck) sweater
7. (crewneck) sweater	**16.** ski cap	**24.** coat
8. parka	**17.** jacket	**25.** rain boots
9. hiking boots		

1. lapel	**9.** wallet	**17.** buckle
2. blazer	**10.** sweatpants	**18.** shopping bag
3. button	**11.** sneakers	**19.** sandal
4. slacks	**12.** sweatband	**20.** collar
5. heel	**13.** tank top	**21.** short sleeve
6. sole	**14.** shorts	**22.** dress
7. shoelace	**15.** long sleeve	**23.** purse
8. sweatshirt	**16.** belt	**24.** umbrella
		25. (high) heels

26. cardigan	**34.** blouse	**42.** loafer
27. (corduroy) pants	**35.** (shoulder) bag	**43.** cap
28. hard hat	**36.** skirt	**44.** glasses
29. T-shirt	**37.** briefcase	**45.** uniform
30. overalls	**38.** raincoat	**46.** shirt
31. lunch box	**39.** vest	**47.** tie
32. (construction) boots	**40.** three-piece suit	**48.** newspaper
33. jacket	**41.** pocket	**49.** shoe

1. undershirt	**8.** half slip	**15.** girdle
2. boxer shorts	**9.** camisole	**16.** knee socks
3. underpants	**10.** full slip	**17.** socks
4. athletic supporter	**11.** (bikini) panties	**18.** slippers
5. pantyhose	**12.** briefs	**19.** pajamas
6. stockings	**13.** bra(ssiere)	**20.** bathrobe
7. long johns	**14.** garter belt	**21.** nightgown

A.	**Jewelry**	13.	tie pin	24.	emery board
1.	earrings	14.	tie clip	25.	nail polish
2.	ring(s)	15.	clip-on earring	26.	eyebrow pencil
3.	engagement ring	16.	pierced earring	27.	perfume
4.	wedding ring	17.	clasp	28.	mascara
5.	chain	18.	post	29.	lipstick
6.	necklace	19.	back	30.	eye shadow
7.	(strand of) beads			31.	nail clippers
8.	pin	B.	**Toiletries and Makeup**	32.	blush
9.	bracelet	20.	razor	33.	eyeliner
10.	watch	21.	after-shave lotion		
11.	watchband	22.	shaving cream		
12.	cuff links	23.	razor blades		

1. short	**9.** light	**16.** closed
2. long	**10.** dark	**17.** striped
3. tight	**11.** high	**18.** checked
4. loose	**12.** low	**19.** polka dot
5. dirty	**13.** new	**20.** solid
6. clean	**14.** old	**21.** print
7. small	**15.** open	**22.** plaid
8. big		

1. rainy
2. cloudy
3. snowy
4. sunny
5. thermometer
6. temperature
7. hot
8. warm
9. cool
10. cold
11. freezing
12. foggy
13. windy
14. dry
15. wet
16. icy

	Spring		**Summer**		**Fall**		**Winter**
1.	paint	5.	water	9.	fill	13.	shovel
2.	clean	6.	mow	10.	rake	14.	sand
3.	dig	7.	pick	11.	chop	15.	scrape
4.	plant	8.	trim	12.	push	16.	carry

A.   Ranch House
1. driveway
2. garage
3. TV antenna
4. roof
5. deck

B.   Colonial-style House
6. porch
7. window
8. shutter
9. chimney

C.   The Backyard
10. gutter
11. hammock
12. lawn mower
13. sprinkler
14. garden hose
15. grass
16. watering can
17. patio
18. drainpipe
19. screen
20. mitt

21. spatula
22. grill
23. charcoal briquettes
24. lounge chair
25. power saw
26. work gloves
27. trowel
28. toolshed
29. hedge clippers
30. rake
31. shovel
32. wheelbarrow

1. ceiling fan	**11.** banister	**21.** speaker
2. ceiling	**12.** staircase	**22.** bookcase
3. wall	**13.** step	**23.** drapes
4. frame	**14.** desk	**24.** cushion
5. painting	**15.** wall-to-wall carpeting	**25.** sofa
6. vase	**16.** recliner	**26.** coffee table
7. mantel	**17.** remote control	**27.** lampshade
8. fireplace	**18.** television	**28.** lamp
9. fire	**19.** wall unit	**29.** end table
10. log	**20.** stereo system	

1. china	**11.** bread and butter plate	**21.** saucer
2. china closet	**12.** fork	**22.** silverware
3. chandelier	**13.** plate	**23.** sugar bowl
4. pitcher	**14.** napkin	**24.** creamer
5. wine glass	**15.** knife	**25.** salad bowl
6. water glass	**16.** tablecloth	**26.** flame
7. table	**17.** chair	**27.** candle
8. spoon	**18.** coffeepot	**28.** candlestick
9. pepper shaker	**19.** teapot	**29.** buffet
10. salt shaker	**20.** cup	

1. dishwasher	**13.** pot	**24.** mixing bowl
2. dish drainer	**14.** casserole dish	**25.** rolling pin
3. steamer	**15.** canister	**26.** cutting board
4. can opener	**16.** toaster	**27.** counter
5. frying pan	**17.** roasting pan	**28.** teakettle
6. bottle opener	**18.** dish towel	**29.** burner
7. colander	**19.** refrigerator	**30.** stove
8. saucepan	**20.** freezer	**31.** coffeemaker
9. lid	**21.** ice tray	**32.** oven
10. dishwashing liquid	**22.** cabinet	**33.** broiler
11. scouring pad	**23.** microwave oven	**34.** pot holder
12. blender		

1. stir	**7.** break	**12.** steam
2. grate	**8.** beat	**13.** broil
3. open	**9.** cut	**14.** bake
4. pour	**10.** slice	**15.** fry
5. peel	**11.** chop	**16.** boil
6. carve		

1. hook	**11.** air conditioner	**23.** bedspread
2. hanger	**12.** blinds	**24.** footboard
3. closet	**13.** tissues	**25.** light switch
4. jewelry box	**14.** headboard	**26.** phone
5. mirror	**15.** pillowcase	**a.** cord
6. comb	**16.** pillow	**b.** jack
7. hairbrush	**17.** mattress	**27.** night table
8. alarm clock	**18.** box spring	**28.** rug
9. bureau	**19.** (flat) sheet	**29.** floor
10. curtain	**20.** blanket	**30.** chest of drawers
	21. bed	
	22. comforter	

1. shade	**12.** disposable diaper	**23.** walker
2. mobile	**13.** cloth diaper	**24.** swing
3. teddy bear	**14.** stroller	**25.** doll house
4. crib	**15.** smoke detector	**26.** cradle
5. bumper	**16.** rocking chair	**27.** stuffed animal
6. baby lotion	**17.** bottle	**28.** doll
7. baby powder	**18.** nipple	**29.** toy chest
8. baby wipes	**19.** stretchie	**30.** playpen
9. changing table	**20.** bib	**31.** puzzle
10. cotton swab	**21.** rattle	**32.** block
11. safety pin	**22.** pacifier	**33.** potty

1. curtain rod	**12.** bath mat	**23.** hand towel
2. curtain rings	**13.** wastepaper basket	**24.** bath towel
3. shower cap	**14.** medicine chest	**25.** towel rack
4. shower head	**15.** soap	**26.** hair dryer
5. shower curtain	**16.** toothpaste	**27.** tile
6. soap dish	**17.** hot water faucet	**28.** hamper
7. sponge	**18.** cold water faucet	**29.** toilet
8. shampoo	**19.** sink	**30.** toilet paper
9. drain	**20.** nailbrush	**31.** toilet brush
10. stopper	**21.** toothbrush	**32.** scale
11. bathtub	**22.** washcloth	

1. stepladder	12. iron	23. paper towels
2. feather duster	13. ironing board	24. dryer
3. flashlight	14. plunger	25. laundry detergent
4. rags	15. bucket	26. bleach
5. circuit breaker	16. vacuum cleaner	27. fabric softener
6. (sponge) mop	17. attachments	28. laundry
7. broom	18. pipe	29. laundry basket
8. dustpan	19. clothesline	30. washing machine
9. cleanser	20. clothespins	31. garbage can
10. window cleaner	21. spray starch	32. mousetrap
11. (mop) refill	22. lightbulb	

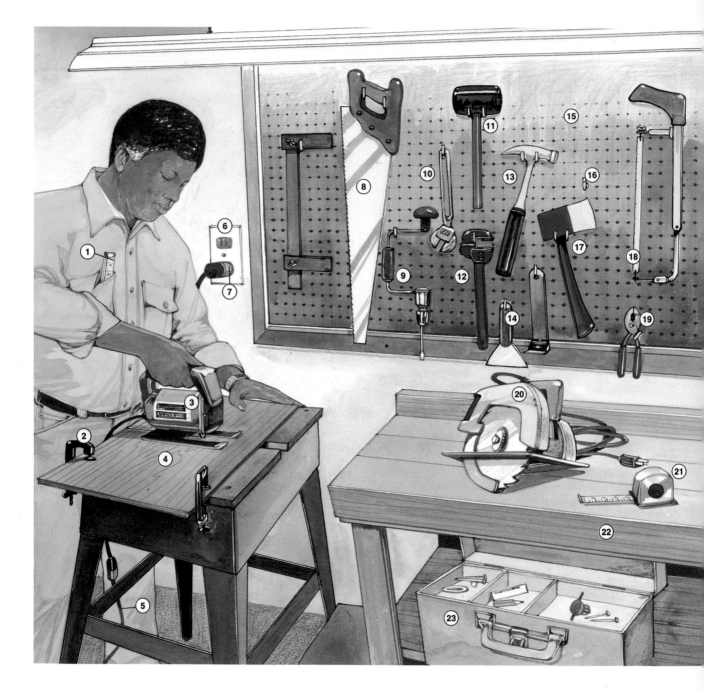

1. carpenter's rule	**9.** brace	**17.** hatchet
2. C-clamp	**10.** wrench	**18.** hacksaw
3. jigsaw	**11.** mallet	**19.** pliers
4. wood	**12.** monkey wrench	**20.** circular saw
5. extension cord	**13.** hammer	**21.** tape measure
6. outlet	**14.** scraper	**22.** workbench
7. grounding plug	**15.** pegboard	**23.** toolbox
8. saw	**16.** hook	

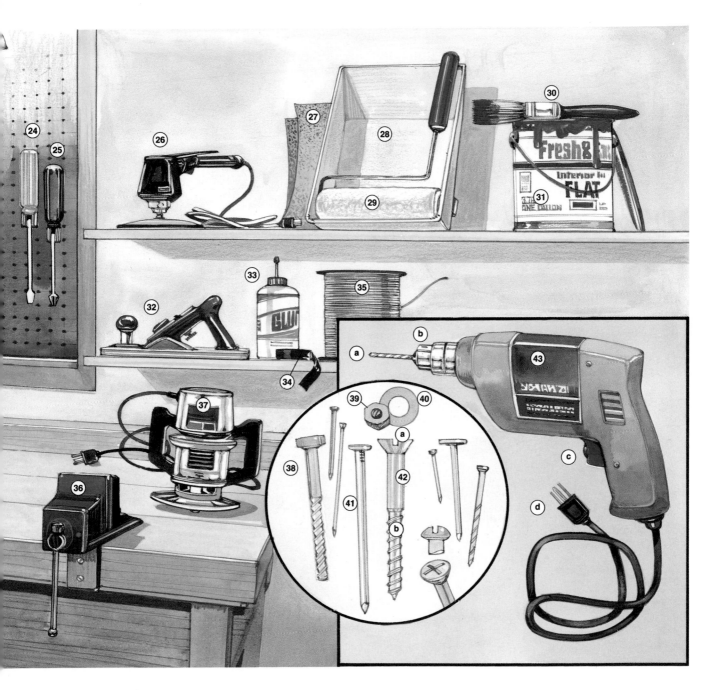

24. screwdriver	**33.** glue	**42.** screw
25. Phillips screwdriver	**34.** electrical tape	**a.** head
26. power sander	**35.** wire	**b.** thread
27. sandpaper	**36.** vise	**43.** electric drill
28. pan	**37.** router	**a.** bit
29. roller	**38.** bolt	**b.** shank
30. paintbrush	**39.** nut	**c.** switch
31. paint	**40.** washer	**d.** plug
32. wood plane	**41.** nail	

1. fold
2. scrub
3. polish
4. tighten
5. wipe
6. hang
7. sweep
8. make (the bed)
9. dry
10. repair
11. iron
12. oil
13. change (the sheets)
14. vacuum
15. dust
16. wash

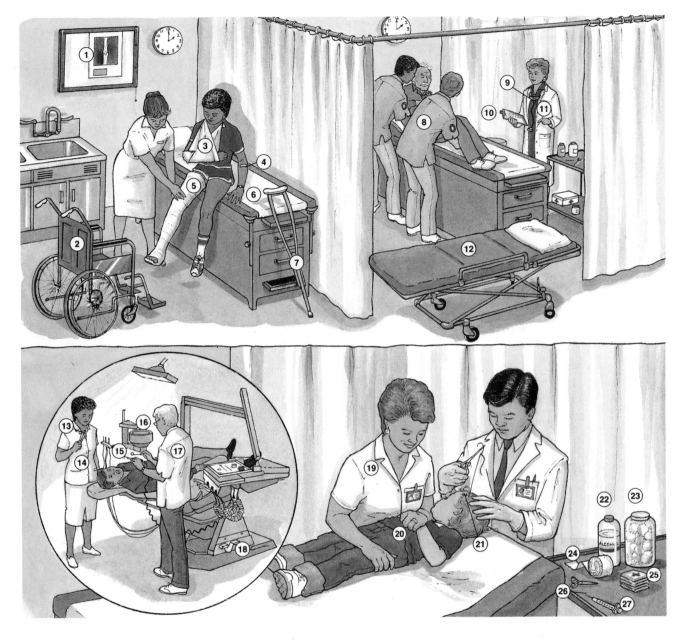

1.	X ray	10.	chart	19.	nurse
2.	wheelchair	11.	doctor	20.	patient
3.	sling	12.	stretcher	21.	stitches
4.	Band-Aid	13.	instruments	22.	alcohol
5.	cast	14.	oral hygienist	23.	cotton balls
6.	examining table	15.	drill	24.	(gauze) bandage
7.	crutch	16.	basin	25.	gauze pads
8.	attendant	17.	dentist	26.	needle
9.	stethoscope	18.	pedal	27.	syringe

1. rash
2. fever
3. insect bite
4. chills
5. black eye
6. headache

7. stomachache
8. backache
9. toothache
10. high blood pressure
11. cold
12. sore throat
    a. tongue depressor

13. sprain
    a. stretch bandage
14. infection
15. broken bone
16. cut
17. bruise
18. burn

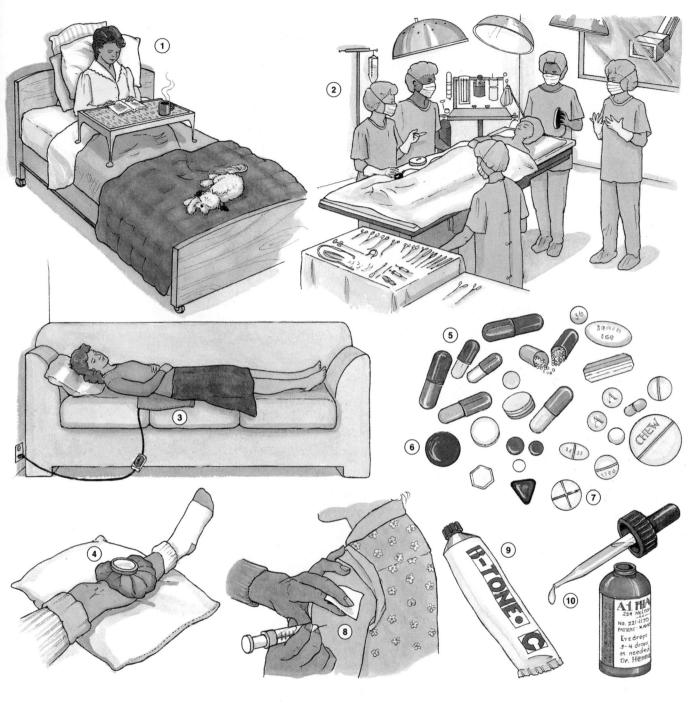

1. bed rest
2. surgery
3. heating pad
4. ice pack

Medicine

5. capsule
6. tablet
7. pill
8. injection
9. ointment
10. eye drops

1. ladder	**7.** paramedic	**13.** coat
2. fire engine	**8.** hose	**14.** axe
3. fire truck	**9.** fire hydrant	**15.** smoke
4. fire escape	**10.** fire fighter	**16.** water
5. fire	**11.** fire extinguisher	**17.** nozzle
6. ambulance	**12.** helmet	

A. **Police Station**	9. nightstick	16. bench
1. jail		17. prosecuting attorney
2. detective	**B.** **Court**	18. witness stand
3. suspect	10. judge	19. court officer
4. handcuffs	11. robes	20. jury box
5. badge	12. gavel	21. jury
6. police officer	13. witness	22. defense attorney
7. gun	14. court reporter	23. defendant
8. holster	15. transcript	24. fingerprints

1. office building	**7.** public telephone	**12.** pedestrian
2. lobby	**8.** street sign	**13.** bus stop
3. corner	**9.** post office	**14.** bench
4. crosswalk	**10.** traffic cop	**15.** trash basket
5. department store	**11.** intersection	**16.** subway station
6. bakery		

17.	elevator	**23.**	apartment house	**28.**	fruit and vegetable market
18.	bookstore	**24.**	building number	**29.**	streetlight
19.	parking garage	**25.**	sidewalk	**30.**	newsstand
20.	parking meter	**26.**	curb	**31.**	street
21.	traffic light	**27.**	baby carriage	**32.**	manhole
22.	drugstore				

A.	**Delivering Mail**		9.	postmark		C.	**Types of Mail**
1.	mailbox		10.	stamp		16.	(airmail) envelope
2.	mail		11.	address		17.	postcard
3.	letter carrier		12.	zip code		18.	money order
4.	mailbag					19.	package
5.	mail truck		B.	**The Post Office**		20.	string
6.	U.S. mailbox		13.	mail slot		21.	label
7.	letter		14.	postal worker		22.	tape
8.	return address		15.	window		23.	Express Mail (package)

1. library clerk	**10.** subject	**19.** globe
2. checkout desk	**11.** row	**20.** atlas
3. library card	**12.** call slip	**21.** reference section
4. card catalog	**13.** microfilm	**22.** information desk
5. drawer	**14.** microfilm reader	**23.** (reference) librarian
6. call card	**15.** periodicals section	**24.** dictionary
7. call number	**16.** magazine	**25.** encyclopedia
8. author	**17.** rack	**26.** shelf
9. title	**18.** photocopy machine	

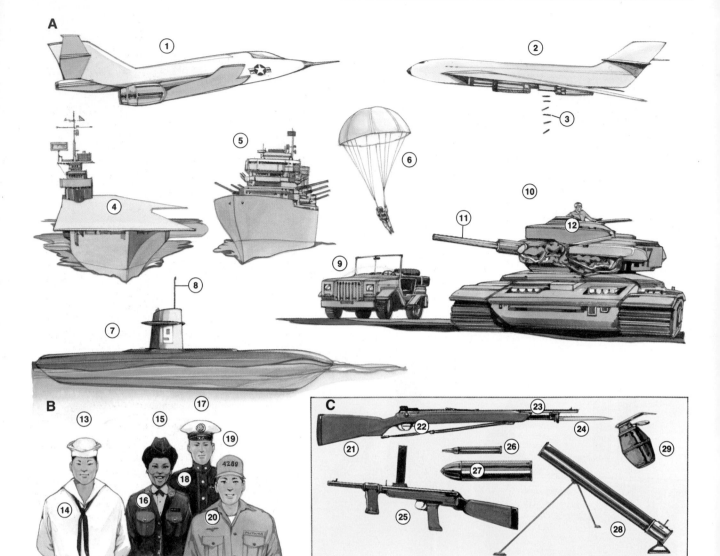

A. Vehicles and Equipment
1. fighter plane
2. bomber
3. bomb
4. aircraft carrier
5. battleship
6. parachute
7. submarine
8. periscope
9. jeep
10. tank
11. cannon
12. gun turret

B. Personnel
13. Navy
14. sailor
15. Army
16. soldier
17. Marines
18. marine
19. Air Force
20. airman

C. Weapons and Ammunition
21. rifle
22. trigger
23. barrel
24. bayonet
25. machine gun
26. bullet
27. shell
28. mortar
29. hand grenade

1. street cleaner	**7.** sanitation worker	**13.** cement truck
2. tow truck	**8.** lunch truck	**14.** dump truck
3. fuel truck	**9.** panel truck	**15.** tractor trailer
4. pickup truck	**10.** delivery person	**16.** truck driver
5. snow plow	**11.** moving van	**17.** transporter
6. garbage truck	**12.** mover	**18.** flatbed

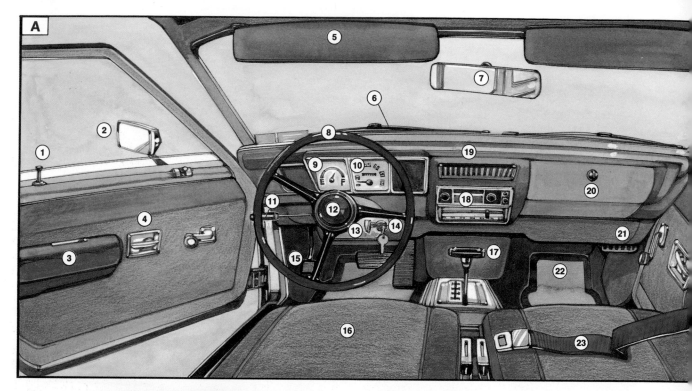

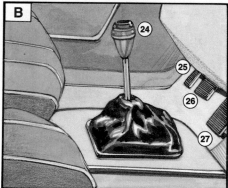

A.	**Automatic Transmission**	14.	ignition	26.	brake
1.	door lock	15.	emergency brake	27.	accelerator
2.	side mirror	16.	bucket seat		
3.	armrest	17.	gearshift	**C.**	**Station Wagon**
4.	door handle	18.	radio	28.	license plate
5.	visor	19.	dashboard	29.	brake light
6.	windshield wiper	20.	glove compartment	30.	back-up light
7.	rearview mirror	21.	vent	31.	taillight
8.	steering wheel	22.	mat	32.	backseat
9.	gas gauge	23.	seat belt	33.	child's seat
10.	speedometer			34.	gas tank
11.	turn signal lever	**B.**	**Manual Transmission**	35.	headrest
12.	horn	24.	stick shift	36.	hubcap
13.	column	25.	clutch	37.	tire

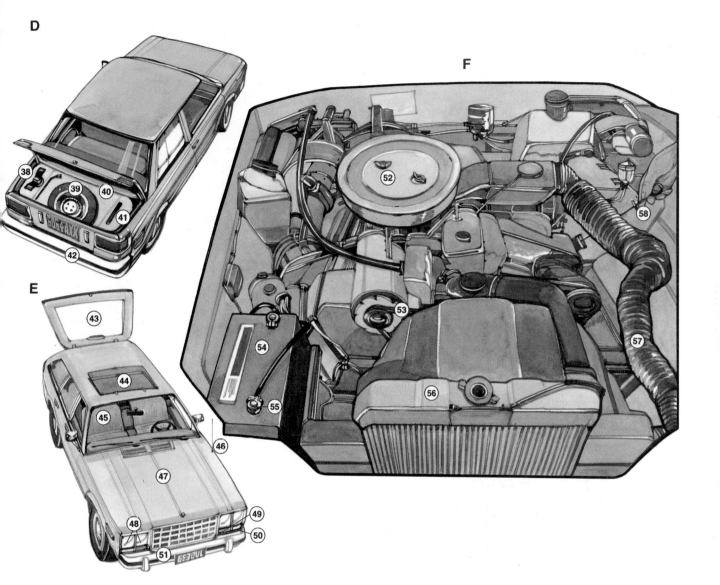

D. (Two-door) Sedan

38. jack
39. spare tire
40. trunk
41. flare
42. rear bumper

E. Four-door Hatchback

43. hatchback
44. sunroof
45. windshield
46. antenna
47. hood
48. headlights
49. parking lights
50. turn signal (lights)
51. front bumper

F. Engine

52. air filter
53. fan belt
54. battery
55. terminal
56. radiator
57. hose
58. dipstick

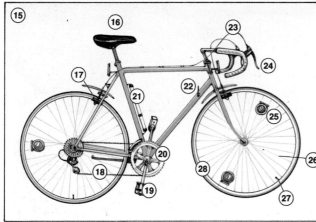

1. training wheels	**12.** touring handlebars	**23.** cable
2. (racing) handlebars	**13.** lock	**24.** hand brake
3. girl's frame	**14.** bike stand	**25.** reflector
4. wheel	**15.** bicycle	**26.** spoke
5. horn	**16.** seat	**27.** valve
6. tricycle	**17.** brake	**28.** tire
7. helmet	**18.** chain	**29.** motor scooter
8. dirt bike	**19.** pedal	**30.** motorcycle
9. kickstand	**20.** sprocket	**31.** shock absorbers
10. fender	**21.** pump	**32.** engine
11. boy's frame	**22.** gear changer	**33.** exhaust pipe

1. interstate highway	**10.** trailer	**19.** motorcycle
2. exit ramp	**11.** service area	**20.** bus
3. overpass	**12.** attendant	**21.** entrance ramp
4. cloverleaf	**13.** air pump	**22.** shoulder
5. left lane	**14.** gas pump	**23.** road sign
6. center lane	**15.** passenger car	**24.** exit sign
7. right lane	**16.** camper	**25.** truck
8. speed limit sign	**17.** sports car	**26.** van
9. hitchhiker	**18.** center divider	**27.** tollbooth

A. Bus
1. cord
2. seat
3. bus driver
4. transfer
5. fare box
6. rider

B. Subway
7. conductor
8. strap
9. car
10. track
11. platform
12. turnstile
13. token booth

C. Train	**D. Taxi**	**E. Other Forms of**
14. commuter train	**21.** fare	**Transportation**
15. engineer	**22.** tip	**29.** monorail
16. ticket	**23.** meter	**30.** streetcar
17. commuter	**24.** receipt	**31.** aerial tramway
18. station	**25.** passenger	**32.** cable car
19. ticket window	**26.** cab driver	**33.** horse-drawn carriage
20. timetable	**27.** taxicab	
	28. taxi stand	

Airport Check-In
1. garment bag
2. carry-on bag
3. traveler
4. ticket
5. porter
6. dolly
7. suitcase
8. baggage

Security
9. security guard
10. metal detector
11. X-ray screener
12. conveyor belt

Boarding
13. cockpit
14. instruments
15. pilot
16. copilot
17. flight engineer
18. boarding pass
19. cabin
20. flight attendant
21. luggage compartment
22. tray table
23. aisle

A.   Aircraft Types
1.   hot air balloon
2.   helicopter
   a.   rotor
3.   private jet
4.   glider

5.   blimp
6.   hang glider
7.   propeller plane
8.   nose
9.   wing
10.   tail

B.   Takeoff
11.   jet engine
12.   cargo area
13.   cargo door
14.   fuselage
15.   landing gear
16.   terminal building
17.   hangar
18.   (jet) plane
19.   runway
20.   control tower

1. fishing boat	**11.** stern	**21.** porthole
2. fisherman	**12.** barge	**22.** deck
3. pier	**13.** tugboat	**23.** windlass
4. forklift	**14.** lighthouse	**24.** anchor
5. bow	**15.** tanker	**25.** line
6. crane	**16.** buoy	**26.** bollard
7. container	**17.** ferry	**27.** ocean liner
8. hold	**18.** smokestack	**28.** dock
9. (container)ship	**19.** lifeboat	**29.** terminal
10. cargo	**20.** gangway	

1. life jacket	**9.** sail	**17.** kayak
2. canoe	**10.** water-skier	**18.** dinghy
3. paddle	**11.** towrope	**19.** mooring
4. sailboat	**12.** outboard motor	**20.** inflatable raft
5. rudder	**13.** motorboat	**21.** oarlock
6. centerboard	**14.** windsurfer	**22.** oar
7. boom	**15.** sailboard	**23.** rowboat
8. mast	**16.** cabin cruiser	

Flowers

1. tulip
   a. stem
2. pansy
3. lily
4. (chrysanthe)mum
5. daisy
6. marigold
7. petunia
8. daffodil
   a. bulb
9. crocus
10. hyacinth
11. iris
12. orchid
13. zinnia
14. gardenia
15. poinsettia
16. violet
17. buttercup
18. rose
    a. bud
    b. petal
    c. thorn
19. sunflower

Grasses and Grains

20. sugarcane
21. rice
22. wheat
23. oats
24. corn

Trees

25. redwood
26. palm
27. eucalyptus
28. dogwood
29. magnolia
30. poplar
31. willow
32. birch
33. oak
   a. twig
   b. acorn

34. pine
   a. needle
   b. cone
35. tree
   a. branch
   b. trunk
   c. bark
   d. root
36. elm
   a. leaf
37. holly
38. maple

Other Plants

39. house plants
40. cactus
41. bushes
42. vine

Poisonous Plants

43. poison oak
44. poison sumac
45. poison ivy

1. snail
   a. shell
   b. antenna
2. oyster
3. mussel
4. slug

5. squid
6. octopus
7. starfish
8. shrimp
9. crab
10. scallop

11. worm
12. jellyfish
   a. tentacle
13. lobster
   a. claw

1. caterpillar
2. cocoon
3. butterfly
4. dragonfly
   a. wing
5. cricket
6. grasshopper
7. mantis

8. scorpion
   a. sting
9. cockroach
10. beetle
11. termite
12. ant
13. mosquito
14. ladybug

15. web
16. spider
17. firefly
18. fly
19. bee
20. wasp
21. moth
22. centipede

1. pigeon	**10.** sparrow	**22.** chick
a. wing	**11.** cardinal	**23.** chicken
2. hummingbird	**12.** ostrich	**24.** pelican
3. crow	**13.** egg	**a.** bill
a. beak	**14.** canary	**25.** duck
4. sea gull	**15.** parakeet	**26.** goose
5. eagle	**16.** parrot	**27.** penguin
6. owl	**17.** woodpecker	**28.** swan
7. hawk	**18.** peacock	**29.** flamingo
a. feather	**19.** pheasant	**30.** stork
8. blue jay	**20.** turkey	**31.** nest
9. robin	**21.** rooster	**32.** roadrunner

A. **Fish**
1. sea horse
2. trout
3. swordfish
   a. tail
   b. fin
   c. gill
4. eel
5. shark

6. stingray
7. flounder

B. **Amphibians and Reptiles**
8. alligator
9. (garter) snake
10. rattlesnake
11. cobra

12. turtle
13. iguana
14. salamander
15. lizard
16. tadpole
17. frog
18. tortoise
   a. shell

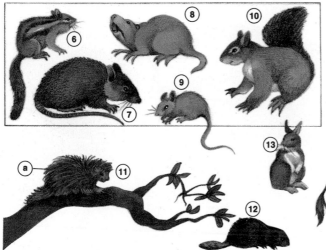

Pouched, Toothless, or Flying Mammals

1. koala
2. armadillo
3. kangaroo
   a. tail
   b. hind legs
   c. pouch
   d. forelegs
4. bat
5. anteater

Rodents

6. chipmunk
7. rat
8. gopher
9. mouse
10. squirrel
11. porcupine
    a. quill
12. beaver
13. rabbit

Hoofed Mammals

14. hippopotamus
15. llama
16. rhinoceros
    a. horn
17. elephant
    a. trunk
    b. tusk
18. zebra

19. bison	**25.** sheep	**32.** cow
20. pony	**26.** deer	**33.** camel
21. horse	**27.** fawn	**a.** hump
a. mane	**28.** goat	**34.** bull
22. foal	**29.** giraffe	**35.** moose
23. donkey	**30.** hog	**a.** antler
24. lamb	**31.** calf	**b.** hoof

1. leopard	**5.** kitten	**Aquatic Mammals**
2. tiger	**6.** fox	**9.** whale
a. claw	**7.** raccoon	**10.** otter
3. lion	**8.** skunk	**11.** walrus
4. cat		**12.** seal
		a. flipper
		13. dolphin

Primates	**Bears**	**Dogs**
14. monkey	20. panda	24. spaniel
15. gibbon	21. black bear	25. terrier
16. chimpanzee	22. polar bear	26. retriever
17. gorilla	23. grizzly bear	27. puppy
18. orangutan		28. shepherd
19. baboon		
		29. wolf
		a. paw
		30. hyena

Continents

1. North America
2. South America
3. Europe
4. Africa
5. Asia
6. Australia
7. Antarctica

Oceans

8. Arctic
9. North Pacific
10. South Pacific
11. North Atlantic
12. South Atlantic
13. Indian
14. Antarctic

Seas, Gulfs, and Bays

15. Beaufort Sea
16. Baffin Bay
17. Gulf of Alaska
18. Hudson Bay
19. Gulf of Mexico

20. Caribbean Sea
21. North Sea
22. Baltic Sea
23. Barents Sea
24. Mediterranean Sea
25. Gulf of Guinea
26. Black Sea
27. Caspian Sea
28. Persian Gulf
29. Red Sea

30. Arabian Sea
31. Kara Sea
32. Bay of Bengal
33. Laptev Sea
34. Bering Sea
35. Sea of Okhotsk
36. Sea of Japan
37. Yellow Sea
38. East China Sea
39. South China Sea

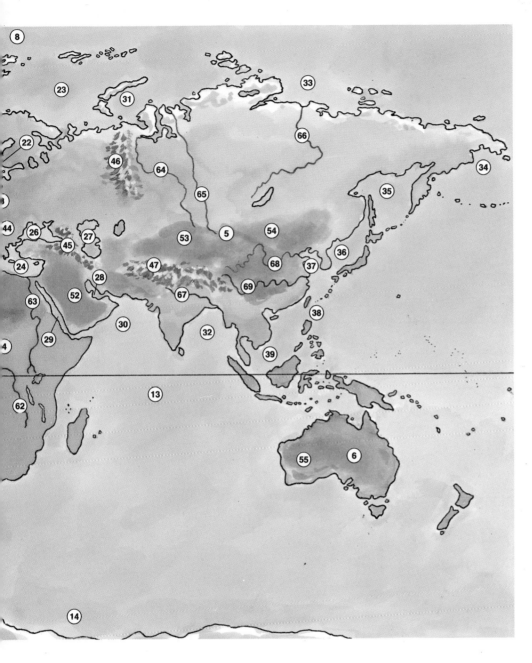

Rivers

56. Yukon
57. Rio Grande
58. Mississippi
59. Amazon
60. Paraná
61. Niger
62. Congo
63. Nile
64. Ob
65. Yenisey
66. Lena
67. Ganges
68. Huang
69. Yangtze

70. equator
71. north
72. south
73. east
74. west

Mountain Ranges

40. Rocky Mountains
41. Appalachian Mountains
42. Sierra Madre
43. Andes
44. Alps
45. Caucasus
46. Urals
47. Himalayas

Deserts

48. Mojave
49. Painted
50. Atacama
51. Sahara
52. Rub' al Khali
53. Takla Makan
54. Gobi
55. Great Sandy

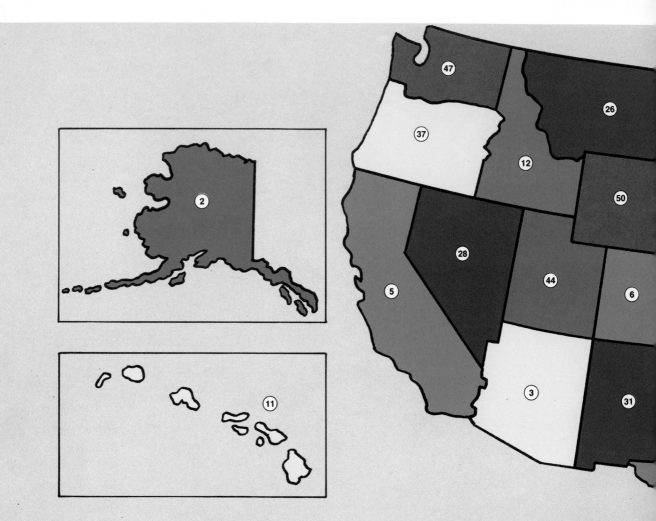

1. Alabama
2. Alaska
3. Arizona
4. Arkansas
5. California
6. Colorado
7. Connecticut
8. Delaware

9. Florida
10. Georgia
11. Hawaii
12. Idaho
13. Illinois
14. Indiana
15. Iowa
16. Kansas

17. Kentucky
18. Louisiana
19. Maine
20. Maryland
21. Massachusetts
22. Michigan
23. Minnesota
24. Mississippi

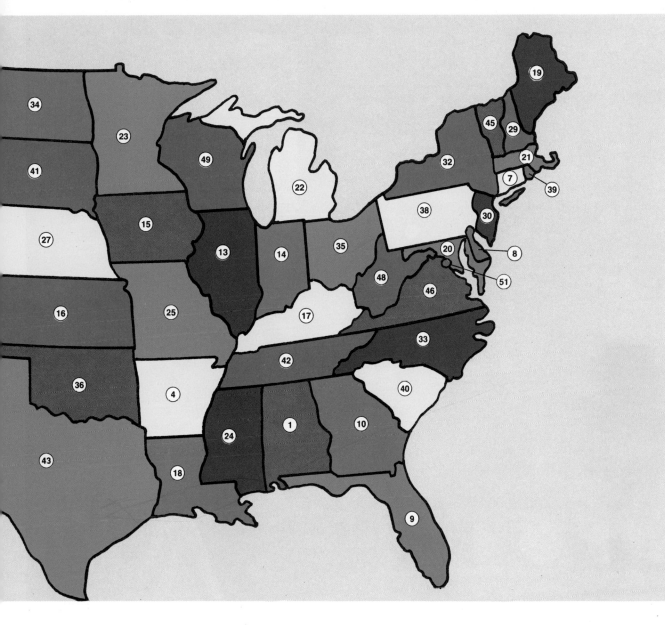

25. Missouri	**34.** North Dakota	**43.** Texas
26. Montana	**35.** Ohio	**44.** Utah
27. Nebraska	**36.** Oklahoma	**45.** Vermont
28. Nevada	**37.** Oregon	**46.** Virginia
29. New Hampshire	**38.** Pennsylvania	**47.** Washington
30. New Jersey	**39.** Rhode Island	**48.** West Virginia
31. New Mexico	**40.** South Carolina	**49.** Wisconsin
32. New York	**41.** South Dakota	**50.** Wyoming
33. North Carolina	**42.** Tennessee	
		51. District of Columbia

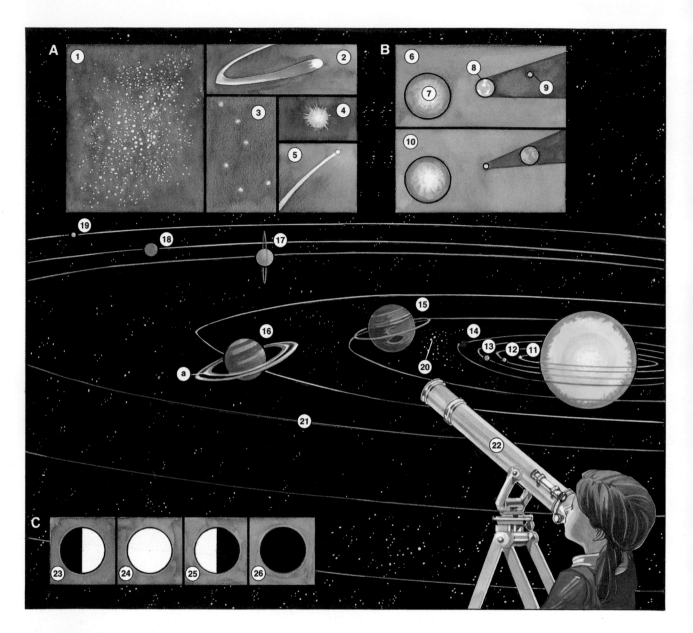

A. **Outer Space**
1. galaxy
2. comet
3. (Big Dipper) constellation
4. star
5. meteor

B. **The Solar System**
6. lunar eclipse
7. Sun
8. Earth

9. Moon
10. solar eclipse
The Planets
11. Mercury
12. Venus
13. Earth
14. Mars
15. Jupiter
16. Saturn
   a. ring
17. Uranus

18. Neptune
19. Pluto

20. asteroid
21. orbit
22. telescope

C. **Phases of the Moon**
23. first quarter
24. full moon
25. last quarter
26. new moon

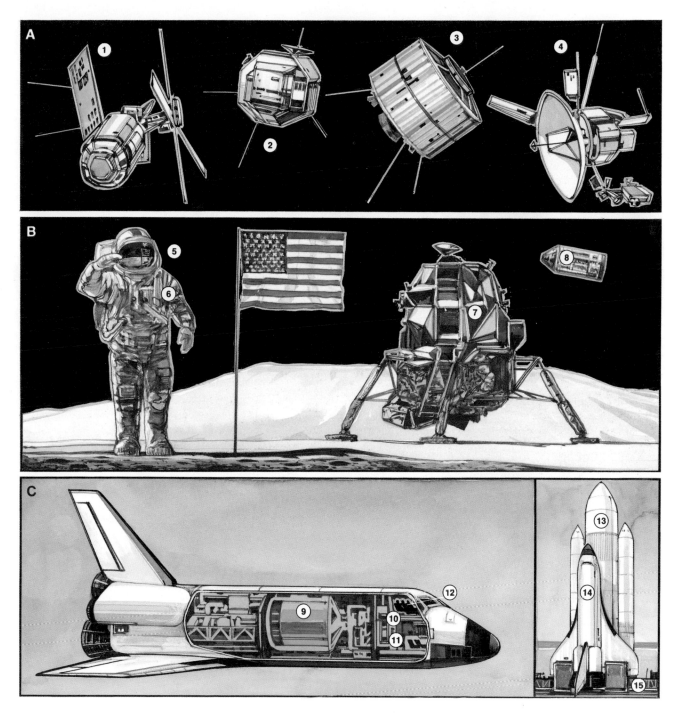

A.   Spacecraft
1. space station
2. communication satellite
3. weather satellite
4. space probe

B.   Landing on the Moon
5. astronaut
6. space suit
7. lunar module
8. command module

C.   The Space Shuttle
9. cargo bay
10. flight deck
11. living quarters
12. crew
13. rocket
14. space shuttle
15. launchpad

1. flag	**10.** chalk	**19.** student
2. clock	**11.** eraser	**20.** pencil sharpener
3. loudspeaker	**12.** hall	**21.** pencil eraser
4. teacher	**13.** (loose-leaf) paper	**22.** ballpoint pen
5. chalkboard	**14.** ring binder	**23.** ruler
6. locker	**15.** spiral notebook	**24.** pencil
7. bulletin board	**16.** desk	**25.** thumbtack
8. computer	**17.** glue	**26.** (text)book
9. chalk tray	**18.** brush	**27.** overhead projector

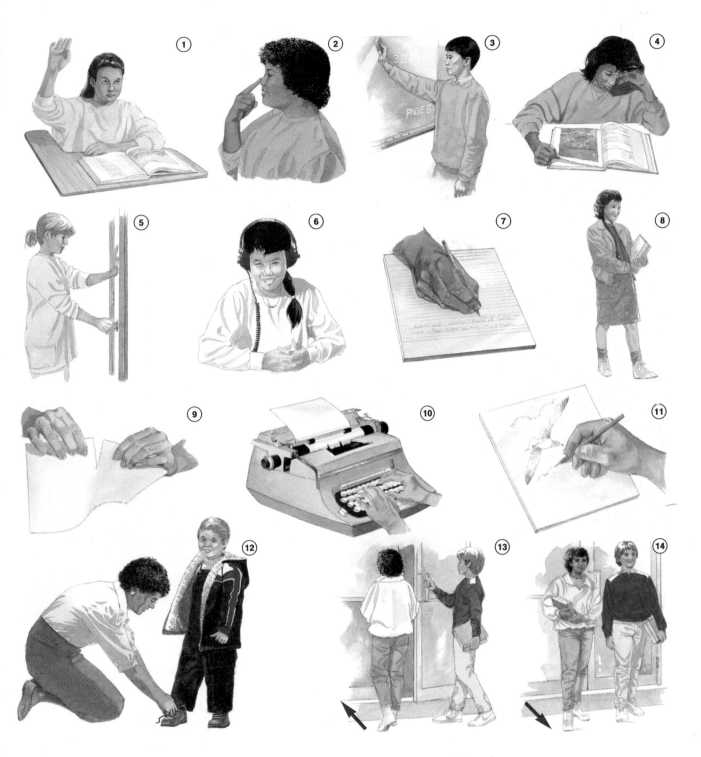

1. raise (one's hand)
2. touch
3. erase
4. read
5. close
6. listen
7. write
8. walk
9. tear
10. type
11. draw
12. tie
13. leave
14. enter

1. prism	**13.** timer	**25.** graduated cylinder
2. flask	**14.** pipette	**26.** medicine dropper
3. petri dish	**15.** magnifying glass	**27.** magnet
4. scale	**16.** filter paper	**28.** forceps
5. weights	**17.** funnel	**29.** tongs
6. wire mesh screen	**18.** rubber tubing	**30.** microscope
7. clamp	**19.** ring stand	**31.** slide
8. rack	**20.** Bunsen burner	**32.** tweezers
9. test tube	**21.** flame	**33.** dissection kit
10. stopper	**22.** thermometer	**34.** stool
11. graph paper	**23.** beaker	
12. safety glasses	**24.** bench	

A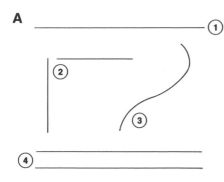

B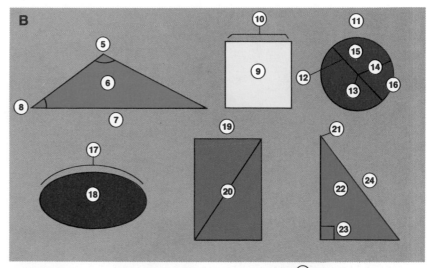

C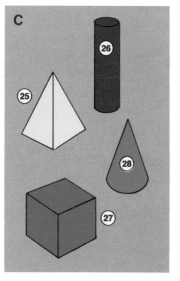

D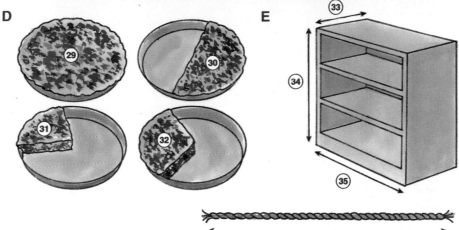

E

A.	**Lines**	13.	center	26.	cylinder
1.	straight line	14.	radius	27.	cube
2.	perpendicular lines	15.	section	28.	cone
3.	curve	16.	arc		
4.	parallel lines	17.	circumference	**D.**	**Fractions**
		18.	oval	29.	whole
B.	**Geometrical Figures**	19.	rectangle	30.	a half (1/2)
5.	obtuse angle	20.	diagonal	31.	a quarter (1/4)
6.	triangle	21.	apex	32.	a third (1/3)
7.	base	22.	right triangle		
8.	acute angle	23.	right angle	**E.**	**Measurement**
9.	square	24.	hypotenuse	33.	depth
10.	side			34.	height
11.	circle	**C.**	**Solid Figures**	35.	width
12.	diameter	25.	pyramid	36.	length

A. Sources of Power

1. oil well
2. derrick
3. sun
4. wind
5. geyser
6. coal mine
7. coal
8. shuttle car
9. elevator
10. shaft
11. waterfall

B. Generation of Power

12. refinery
13. nuclear reactor
14. core
15. uranium rods
16. cooling tower
17. solar collector
18. dam
19. windmill
20. power station
21. electrical generator
22. smokestack
23. transmission towers
24. power lines
25. transformer
26. utility pole

C. Uses and Products

27. heat
28. gas(oline)
29. natural gas
30. propane gas
31. jet fuel
32. electricity
33. motor oil
34. diesel fuel

A. Dairy Farm	10. sheep	18. row
1. orchard	11. dairy cow	19. scarecrow
2. fruit tree		
3. farmhouse	**B. Wheat Farm**	**C. Ranch**
4. silo	12. livestock	20. (herd of) cattle
5. barn	13. (bale of) hay	21. cowboy
6. pasture	14. pitchfork	22. cowgirl
7. farmer	15. tractor	23. horses
8. barnyard	16. (wheat) field	24. corral
9. fence	17. combine	25. trough

A.	**Construction Site**	
1.	rafters	
2.	shingle	
3.	level	
4.	hard hat	
5.	builder	
6.	blueprints	
7.	scaffolding	
8.	ladder	
9.	rung	
10.	cement	

11.	foundation
12.	bricks
13.	pickax
14.	construction worker
15.	shovel
16.	board
17.	linesman
18.	cherry picker

B.	**Road Work**
19.	cone
20.	flag
21.	barricade
22.	jackhammer
23.	wheelbarrow
24.	center divider
25.	cement mixer
26.	backhoe
27.	bulldozer

1. switchboard operator	**12.** in-box	**23.** file clerk
2. headset	**13.** desk	**24.** photocopier
3. switchboard	**14.** rolodex	**25.** message pad
4. printer	**15.** telephone	**26.** (legal) pad
5. cubicle	**16.** computer	**27.** stapler
6. typist	**17.** typing chair	**28.** paper clips
7. word processor	**18.** manager	**29.** staple remover
8. printout	**19.** calculator	**30.** pencil sharpener
9. calendar	**20.** bookcase	**31.** envelope
10. typewriter	**21.** file cabinet	
11. secretary	**22.** file folder	

1. pharmacist	**6.** tailor	**11.** florist
2. mechanic	**7.** greengrocer	**12.** jeweller
3. barber	**8.** baker	**13.** butcher
4. travel agent	**9.** optician	
5. repairperson	**10.** hairdresser	

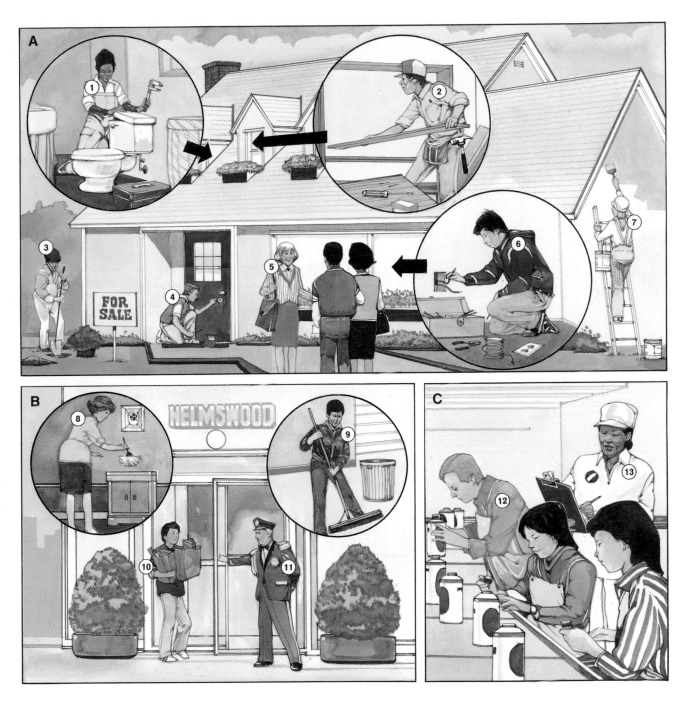

A. Repair and Maintenance
1. plumber
2. carpenter
3. gardener
4. locksmith
5. real estate agent
6. electrician
7. painter

B. Household Services
8. housekeeper
9. janitor
10. delivery boy
11. doorman

C. Factory Work
12. shop worker
13. foreman

A.   Media and Arts
1.   weather forecaster
2.   newscaster
3.   artist
4.   photographer
5.   model
6.   fashion designer
7.   writer

8.   architect
9.   disc jockey (DJ)
10.   cameraperson
11.   reporter
12.   salesperson

B.   Banking
13.   officer

14.   security guard
15.   teller

C.   Business Workers
16.   computer programmer
17.   receptionist
18.   accountant
19.   messenger

1. zoo	**8.** (duck) pond	**15.** playground
2. band shell	**9.** jogging path	**16.** swings
3. vendor	**10.** bench	**17.** jungle gym
4. hand truck	**11.** trash can	**18.** seesaw
5. merry-go-round	**12.** slide	**19.** water fountain
6. horseback rider	**13.** sandbox	
7. bridle path	**14.** sprinkler	

1. plateau
2. hikers
3. canyon
4. hill
5. park ranger

Fishing

6. stream
7. fishing rod
8. fishing line
9. fishing net
10. waders
11. rocks

Picnic Area

12. grill
13. picnic basket
14. thermos
15. picnic table

Rafting
16. raft
17. rapids
18. waterfall

Mountain Climbing
19. mountain
20. peak
21. cliff
22. harness
23. rope

Camping
24. tent
25. camp stove
26. sleeping bag
27. gear
28. frame backpack
29. lantern
30. stake
31. campfire
32. woods

1. boardwalk
2. refreshment stand
3. motel
4. biker
5. whistle
6. lifeguard
7. binoculars
8. lifeguard chair
9. life preserver
10. lifeboat
11. beach ball
12. sand dunes
13. Frisbee™
14. sunglasses
15. beach towel
16. pail
17. shovel
18. bathing suit
19. sunbather
20. beach chair
21. beach umbrella

22.	kite	**29.**	tube	**36.**	flippers
23.	runners	**30.**	water	**37.**	scuba tank
24.	wave	**31.**	sand	**38.**	wet suit
25.	surfboard	**32.**	sandcastle	**39.**	suntan lotion
26.	air mattress	**33.**	bathing trunks	**40.**	shell
27.	kickboard	**34.**	snorkel	**41.**	cooler
28.	swimmer	**35.**	mask		

Baseball
1. umpire
2. catcher
3. catcher's mask
4. catcher's mitt
5. bat
6. batting helmet
7. batter

Little League Baseball
8. Little Leaguer
9. uniform

Softball
10. softball
11. cap
12. glove

Football
13. football
14. helmet

Lacrosse
15. face guard
16. lacrosse stick

Ice Hockey
17. puck
18. hockey stick

Basketball
19. backboard
20. basket
21. basketball

Volleyball
22. volleyball
23. net

Soccer
24. goalie
25. goal
26. soccer ball

A. Baseball Diamond	**13.** dugout	**24.** split end
1. left fielder	**14.** batter	**25.** left tackle
2. center fielder	**15.** home plate	**26.** left guard
3. right fielder	**16.** catcher	**27.** center
4. third baseman	**17.** umpire	**28.** right guard
5. shortstop	**18.** batboy	**29.** right tackle
6. base		**30.** tight end
7. second baseman	**B. Football Field**	**31.** flanker
8. first baseman	**19.** scoreboard	**32.** quarterback
9. foul line	**20.** cheerleaders	**33.** halfback
10. stands	**21.** coach	**34.** fullback
11. pitcher's mound	**22.** referee	**35.** goalpost
12. pitcher	**23.** end zone	

Tennis
1. tennis ball
2. racket

Bowling
3. gutter
4. lane
5. pin
6. bowling ball

Golf
7. golf ball
8. hole
9. putter
10. golfer

Handball
11. glove
12. handball
13. court

Boxing
14. head protector
15. glove
16. referee
17. ring

Ping-Pong
18. paddle
19. ping-pong ball

Horse Racing
20. saddle
21. jockey
22. reins

Gymnastics
23. gymnast
24. balance beam

Ice Skating
25. rink
26. skate
27. blade

Racquetball
28. safety goggles
29. racquet
30. racquetball

Track and Field
31. runner
32. track

Cross-Country Skiing
33. skis
34. pole
35. skier

A. Tennis Court	**8.** golf cart	**16.** binding
1. service court	**9.** flag	**17.** ski
2. net	**10.** green	**18.** ski lift
3. service line	**11.** sand trap	
4. baseline	**12.** fairway	**D. Race Track**
	13. tee	**19.** stretch
B. Golf Course		**20.** starting gate
5. clubs		**21.** finish line
6. rough	**C. Ski Slope**	
7. golf bag	**14.** pole	
	15. ski boot	

1. hit	**4.** catch	**7.** fall
2. serve	**5.** pass	**8.** jump
3. kick	**6.** run	

9. skate	**12.** surf	**15.** drive
10. throw	**13.** ride	**16.** shoot
11. bounce	**14.** dive	

Strings

1. piano
   a. keyboard
2. sheet music
3. ukulele
4. mandolin
5. banjo
6. harp
7. violin
   a. bow
8. viola
9. cello
10. bass
   a. string

11. guitar
   a. pick

Woodwinds

12. piccolo
13. flute
14. bassoon
15. oboe
16. clarinet

Percussion

17. tambourine
18. cymbals
19. drum
   a. drumsticks
20. conga

21. kettledrum
22. bongos

Brass

23. trombone
24. saxophone
25. trumpet
26. French horn
27. tuba

Other Instruments

28. accordion
29. organ
30. harmonica
31. xylophone

A. The Ballet
1. curtain
2. scenery
3. dancer
4. spotlight
5. stage
6. orchestra
7. podium
8. conductor
9. baton
10. musician

11. box seat
12. orchestra seating
13. mezzanine
14. balcony
15. audience
16. usher
17. programs

B. Musical Comedy
18. chorus
19. actor
20. actress

C. Rock Group
21. synthesizer
22. keyboard player
23. bass guitarist
24. singer
25. lead guitarist
26. electric guitar
27. drummer

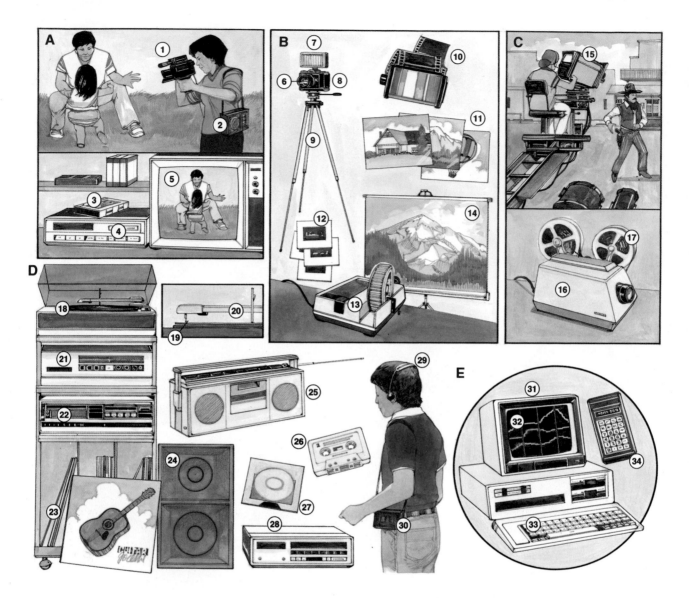

A. Video	**12.** slides	**23.** records
1. video camera	**13.** slide projector	**24.** speaker
2. Minicam™	**14.** screen	**25.** stereo cassette player
3. videocassette (tape)		**26.** cassette
4. VCR (videocassette recorder)	**C. Film**	**27.** compact disc (CD)
5. television	**15.** movie camera	**28.** compact disc player
	16. projector	**29.** headphones
B. Photography	**17.** (reel of) film	**30.** Sony Walkman
6. lens		
7. flash	**D. Audio**	**E. Computers**
8. camera	**18.** turntable	**31.** personal computer (PC)
9. tripod	**19.** cartridge needle	**32.** monitor
10. (roll of) film	**20.** arm	**33.** keyboard
11. prints	**21.** receiver	**34.** calculator
	22. cassette deck	

A.	**Sewing**	11.	hem	B.	**Other Needlecrafts**
1.	sewing machine	12.	hem binding	22.	knitting
2.	(spool of) thread	13.	snap	23.	wool
3.	pincushion	14.	hook and eye	24.	skein
4.	material	15.	tape measure	25.	knitting needle
5.	pinking shears	16.	zipper	26.	needlepoint
6.	pattern piece	17.	(pair of) scissors	27.	embroidery
7.	pattern	18.	needle	28.	crochet
8.	buttonhole	19.	stitch	29.	crochet hook
9.	button	20.	pin	30.	weaving
10.	seam	21.	thimble	31.	yarn
				32.	quilting

1. at (the window)
2. above (the black cat)
3. below (the white cat)
4. between (the pillows)
5. on (the rug)
6. in front of (the fireplace)
7. in (the drawer)
8. under (the desk)
9. behind (the chair)
10. on top of (the table)
11. next to (the TV)

1.	through (the lighthouse)	**5.**	away from (the hole)	**9.**	to (the course)
2.	around (the lighthouse)	**6.**	across (the water)	**10.**	from (the course)
3.	down (the hill)	**7.**	out of (the water)	**11.**	up (the hill)
4.	toward (the hole)	**8.**	over (the bridge)	**12.**	into (the hole)

Days of the Week

Sunday
Monday
Tuesday
Wednesday
Thursday
Friday
Saturday

Months of the Year

January
February
March
April
May
June
July
August
September
October
November
December

Numbers

0	zero
1	one
2	two
3	three
4	four
5	five
6	six
7	seven
8	eight
9	nine
10	ten
11	eleven
12	twelve
13	thirteen
14	fourteen
15	fifteen
16	sixteen
17	seventeen
18	eighteen
19	nineteen
20	twenty
21	twenty-one
30	thirty
40	forty
50	fifty
60	sixty
70	seventy
80	eighty
90	ninety
100	a/one hundred
500	five hundred
621	six hundred (and) twenty-one
1,000	a/one thousand
1,000,000	a/one million

Colors

red
green
blue
pink
yellow
purple
white
brown
black
orange
gray

Two numbers occur after words in the index: the first refers to the page where the word is illustrated and the second to the item number of the word on that page. For example, above [ə bŭv/] **102** 2 means that the word *above* is the item numbered 2 on page 102. If only a bold number appears, then that word is part of the unit title or a subtitle.

The index includes a pronunciation guide for all the words illustrated in the book. This guide uses symbols commonly found in dictionaries for native speakers. These symbols, unlike those used in transcription systems such as the International Phonetic Alphabet, tend to preserve spelling and so should help you to become more aware of the connections between written English and spoken English.

Consonants

[b] as in **back** [băk]	[k] as in **kite** [kīt]	[sh] as in **shell** [shĕl]
[ch] as in **cheek** [chēk]	[l] as in **leaf** [lēf]	[t] as in **tape** [tāp]
[d] as in **date** [dāt]	[m] as in **man** [măn]	[th] as in **three** [thrē]
[dh] as in **the** [dh]	[n] as in **neck** [nĕk]	[v] as in **vine** [vīn]
[f] as in **face** [fās]	[ng] as in **ring** [rĭng]	[w] as in **waist** [wāst]
[g] as in **gas** [găs]	[p] as in **pack** [păk]	[y] as in **yam** [yăm]
[h] as in **half** [hăf]	[r] as in **rake** [rāk]	[z] as in **zoo** [zo͞o]
[j] as in **jack** [jăk]	[s] as in **sand** [sănd]	[zh] as in **measure** [mĕzh/ ər]

Vowels

[ā] as in **bake** [bāk]	[ī] as in **lime** [līm]	[o͞o] as in **cool** [ko͞ol]
[ă] as in **back** [băk]	[ĭ] as in **lip** [lĭp]	[o͝o] as in **book** [bo͝ok]
[ä] as in **bar** [bär]	[ï] as in **beer** [bïr]	[ow] as in **cow** [kow]
[ē] as in **beat** [bēt]	[ō] as in **post** [pōst]	[oy] as in **boy** [boy]
[ĕ] as in **bed** [bĕd]	[ŏ] as in **box** [bŏks]	[ŭ] as in **cut** [kŭt]
[ë] as in **bear** [bër]	[ö] as in **claw** [klö]	[ü] as in **curb** [kürb]
	or **for** [för]	[ə] as in **above** [ə bŭv/]

All pronunciation symbols used are alphabetical except for the schwa [ə], which is the most frequent vowel sound in English. If you use it appropriately in unstressed syllables, your pronunciation will sound more natural.

You should note that an umlaut ([¨]) calls attention to the special quality of vowels before [r]. (The sound [ö] can also represent a vowel not followed by [r] as in *claw.*) You should listen carefully to native speakers to discover how these vowels actually sound.

Stress

This guide also follows the system for marking stress used in many dictionaries for native speakers.
   (1) Stress is not marked if a word consisting of a single syllable occurs in isolation.
   (2) Where stress is marked, two levels are distinguished:
      a bold accent [**/**] is placed after each syllable with primary stress,
      a light accent [/] is placed after each syllable with secondary stress.

Syllable Boundaries

Syllable boundaries are indicated by a single space.

NOTE: The pronunciation used in this index is based on patterns of American English. There has been no attempt to represent all of the varieties of American English. Students should listen to native speakers to hear how the language actually sounds in a particular region.

above [ə bŭv′] **102** 2

abdomen [ăb′də mən] **4** 14

accelerator [ăk sĕl′ə rā′tər] **50** 27

accordion [ə kör′dē ən] **98** 28

accountant [ə kown′tənt] **86** 18

acorn [ā′körn] **61** 33b

acorn squash [ā′körn skwŏsh′] **7** 28

across [ə krös′] **103** 6

actor [ăk′tər] **99** 19

actress [ăk′trəs] **99** 20

acute angle [ə kyoōt′ăng′gəl] **79** 8

address [ă′drĕs] **46** 11

adjectives [ăj′ĭk tĭvz] **24, 25**

aerial tramway [ër′ē əl trăm′wā] **55** 31

Africa [ă′frĭ kə] **70** 4

after-shave lotion [ăf′tər shāv lō′shən]
    23 21

ailments [āl′mənts] **40**

air conditioner [ër′kən dĭ′shə nər]
    32 11

air filter [ër′fĭl′tər] **51** 52

Air Force [ër′förs′] **48** 19

air mattress [ër′mă′trəs] **91** 26

air pump [ër′ pŭmp′] **53** 13

air travel [ër′ tră′vəl] **56**

aircraft [ër′krăft′] **57**

aircraft carrier [ër′krăft kăr′yər] **48** 4

aircraft types [ër′krăft tīps′] **57**

(airmail) envelope
    [ër′māl ĕn′və lōp] **46** 16

airman [ër′mən] **48** 20

airport check-in [ër′pört chĕk′ĭn] **56**

aisle [ī′əl] **14** 10, **56** 23

Alabama [ăl′ə bă′mə] **72** 1

alarm clock [ə lärm′ klŏk] **32** 8

Alaska [ə lăs′kə] **72** 2

alcohol [ăl′kə höl′] **39** 22

alligator [ăl′ə gā′tər] **65** 8

almond(s) [ö′mənd(z)] **9** 31

Alps [ălps] **70** 44

Amazon River [ă′mə zŏn rĭv′ər]
    71 59

ambulance [ăm′byə ləns] **42** 6

amphibians [ăm fĭ′bē ənz] **65**

ammunition [ăm′yə nĭsh′ən] **48**

anchor [ăng′kər] **58** 24

Andes [ăn′dēz] **71** 43

ankle [ăng′kəl] **5** 49

animals [ăn′ə məlz] **62-69**

ant [ănt] **63** 12

Antarctic Ocean [ănt ärk′tĭk ō′shən]
    70 14

Antarctica [ănt ärk′tĭ kə] **70** 7

anteater [ănt′ē′tər] **66** 5

antenna [ăn tĕn′ə] **51** 46, **62** 1b

antler [ănt′lər] **67** 35a

apartment house
    [ə pärt′mənt hows′] **45** 23

apex [ā′pĕks] **79** 21

Appalachian Mountains
    [ăp′ə lā′chē ən mown′tənz] **71** 41

apple [ă′pəl] **8** 2

apricot [ăp′rə kŏt′] **9** 25

apron [ā′prən] **16** 6

aquatic mammals
    [ə kwŏ′tĭk mă′məlz] **68**

Arabian Sea [ə rā′bē ən sē′] **70** 30

arc [ärk] **79** 16

architect [är′kə tĕkt′] **86** 8

Arctic [ärk′tĭk] **70** 8

Arizona [ăr′ə zō′nə] **72** 3

Arkansas [är′kən sö′] **72** 4

arm [ärm] **4** 6, **100** 20

armadillo [är′mə dĭl′ō] **66** 2

armed forces [ärmd′ för′səz] **48**

armpit [ärm′pĭt′] **4** 10

armrest [ärm′rĕst′] **50** 3

Army [är′mē] **48** 15

around [ə rownd′] **103** 2

artery [är′tə rē] **5** 69

artichoke [är′tə chōk′] **6** 11

artist [är′təst] **86** 3

arts [ärts] **86**

ashtray [ăsh′trā′] **16** 29

Asia [ā′zhə] **70** 5

asparagus [ə spăr′ə gəs] **6** 18

asteroid [ăs′tə royd′] **74** 20

astronaut [ăs′trə nŏt′] **75** 5

at [ăt] **102** 1

Atacama Desert
    [ăt′ə kŏ′mə dĕz′ərt] **71** 50

athletic supporter
    [ăth lĕ′tĭk sə pör′tər] **22** 4

atlas [ăt′ləs] **47** 20

attachments [ə tăch′mənts] **35** 17

attendant [ə tĕn′dənt] **39** 8, **53** 12

audience [ö′dē əns] **99** 15

audio [ö′dē ō′] **100**

aunt [ănt] **3** 6

Australia [ö strāl′yə] **70** 6

author [ö′thər] **47** 8

automatic transmission
    [ö′ tə mă t′ĭk trănz mĭ′shən] **50**

avocado [ăv′ə kŏ′dō] **9** 33

away from [ə wā′ frŭm] **103** 5

axe [ăks] **42** 14

baboon [bă boon′] **69** 19

baby [bā′ bē] **2** 5

baby carriage [bā′ bē kăr′ĭj] **45** 27

baby lotion [bā′ bē lō′shən] **33** 6

baby powder [bā′ bē pow′dər] **33** 7

baby wipes [bā′ bē wīps′] **33** 8

baby's room [bā′ bēz rōōm′] **33**

back [băk] **4** 11, **23** 19

backache [băk′āk′] **40** 8

backboard [băk′börd′] **92** 19

backhoe [băk′hō′] **82** 26

backpack [băk′păk′] **19** 4

backseat [băk′sēt′] **50** 32

backyard [băk′yärd′] **27**

back-up light [băk′əp līt′] **50** 30

bacon [bā′kən] **10** 11, **18,** 33

badge [băj] **43** 5

Baffin Bay [băf′ən bā′] **70** 16

bag [băg] **12** 8, **15** 25, **21** 35

baggage [băg′ĭj] **56** 8

bake [bāk] **31** 14

baked beans [bākt′ bēnz′] **18** 3

baked goods [bākt goōdz′] **14** 11

baked potato [bākt′ pə tā′tō] **18** 20

baker [bā′kər] **84** 8

bakery [bā′kə rē] **44** 6

balance beam [băl′əns bēm′] **94** 24

balcony [băl′kə nē] **99** 14

(bale of) hay [bāl′ əv hā′] **81** 13

ball [böl] **5** 52

ballet [bă lā′] **99**

ballfields [böl′fēldz′] **93**

ballpoint pen [böl′poynt pĕn′] **76** 22

Baltic Sea [böl′tĭk sē′] **70** 22

bananas [bə nă′nəz] **9** 20

Band-Aid [bănd′ ād′] **39** 4

band shell [bănd′ shĕl′] **87** 2

bandage [băn′dĭj] **39** 24

banister [băn′ə stər] **28** 11

banjo [băn′jō′] **98** 5

banking [băng′kĭng] **86**

bar [bär] **13** 18, **16** 24

bar stool [bär′stool′] **16** 25

barber [bär′bər] **84** 3

Barents Sea [băr′ənts sē′] **70** 23

barge [bärj] **58** 12

bark [bärk] **61** 35c

barn [bärn] **81** 5

barnyard [bärn′yärd′] **81** 8

barrel [băr′əl] **48** 23

barricade [băr′ə kād′] **82** 21

bartender [bär′těn′dər] **16** 21

base [bās] **79** 7, **93** 6

baseball [bās′böl′] **92**

baseball diamond [bās′böl dī′mənd]
93

baseline [bās′līn′] **95** 4

basin [bā′sən] **39** 16

basket [băs′kət] **92** 20

basketball [băs′kət böl′] **92**, **92** 21

bass [bās] **98** 10

bass guitarist [bās′gə tär′əst] **99** 23

bassoon [bă soon′] **98** 14

bat [băt] **66** 4, **92** 5

batboy [băt′boy′] **93** 18

bath mat [băth′ măt′] **34** 12

bath towel [băth′ tow′əl] **34** 24

bathing suit [bā′dhĭng soot′] **90** 18

bathing trunks [bā′ dhĭng trŭngks′]
91 33

bathrobe [băth′ rōb] **22** 20

bathroom [băth′ room′] **34**

bathtub [băth′ tŭb′] **34** 11

baton [bə tŏn′] **99** 9

batter [băt′ ər] **92** 7, **93** 14

battery [băt′ə rē] **51** 54

batting helmet [băt′ĭng hěl′mət] **92** 6

battleship [băt′əl shĭp′] **48** 5

Bay of Bengal [bā′ əv běn göl′] **70** 32

bayonet [bā′ə nět′] **48** 24

bays [bāz] **70**

beach [bēch] **90**

beach ball [bēch′ böl′] **90** 11

beach chair [bēch′ chër′] **90** 20

beach towel [bēch′ tow′ əl] **90** 15

beach umbrella [bēch′əm brěl′ə]
90 21

beads [bēdz] **23** 7

beak [bēk] **64** 3a

beaker [bē′ kər] **78** 23

beard [bïrd] **4** 39

bears [bërz] **69**

beat [bēt] **31** 8

Beaufort Sea [bō′ fərt sē′] **70** 15

beaver [bē′vər] **66** 12

bed [běd] **32** 21

bed rest [běd′ rěst′] **41** 1

bedroom [běd′room′] **32**

bedspread [běd′sprěd′] **32** 23

bee [bē] **63** 19

beef [bēf] **10** 1

beef stew [bēf′ stoo′] **18** 14

beer [bïr] **16** 23

beet(s) [bēts] **7** 33

beetle [bē′təl] **63** 10

behind [bə hīnd′] **102** 9

below [bə lō′] **102** 3

belt [bělt] **20** 16

bench [běnch] **43** 16, **44** 14, **78** 24,
87 10

beret [bə rā′] **19** 22

Bering Sea [bër′ĭng sē′] **70** 34

berries [bër′ēz] **8**

between [bə twēn′] **102** 4

beverages [běv′rə jəz] **14** 14

bib [bĭb] **33** 20

bicycle [bī′sĭ kəl] **52** 15

big [bĭg] **24** 8

(Big Dipper) constellation
[bĭg′ dĭ′pər kŏn stə lā′shən] **74** 3

big toe [bĭg′ tō′] **5** 53

bike stand [bīk′ stănd′] **52** 14

biker [bī′kər] **90** 4

bikes [bīks] **52**

(bikini) panties [bə kē′ nē păn′ tēz]
22 11

bill [bĭl] **64** 24a

bin [bĭn] **15** 16

binding [bīn′ dĭng] **95** 16

binoculars [bə nŏk′ yə lərs] **90** 7

birch [bürch] **61** 32

birds [bürdz] **64**

biscuit [bĭs′ kət] **18** 27

bison [bī′sən] **67** 19

bit [bĭt] **37** 43a

black bear [blăk′ bër′] **69** 21

black bean(s) [blăk′ bēn(z)′] **6** 14

black eye [blăk′ ī′] **40** 5

Black Sea [blăk′ sē′] **70** 26

blackberries [blăk′ bër′ ēz] **8** 12

bladder [blă′ dər] **5** 72

blade [blād] **94** 27

blanket [blăng′ket] **32** 20

blazer [blā′zer] **20** 2

bleach [blēch] **35** 26

blender [blěn′dər] **30** 12

blimp [blĭmp] **57** 5

blinds [blīndz] **32** 12

block [blŏk] **33** 32

blouse [blows] **21** 34

blue jay [bloo′ ja′] **64** 8

(blue) jeans [bloo′ jēnz′] **19** 6

blueberries [bloo′bër′ēz] **8** 14

blueprints [bloo′prĭnts′] **82** 6

blush [blŭsh] **23** 32

board [börd] **82** 16

boarding [bör′dĭng] **56**

boarding pass [bör′dĭng păs′] **56** 18

boardwalk [börd′wök′] **90** 1

body [bŏ′dē] **4**

boil [boyl] **31** 16

bollard [bŏl′ərd] **58** 26

bolt [bōlt] **37** 38

bomb [bŏm] **48** 3

bomber [bŏm′ ər] **48** 2

bongos [bŏng′ gōz] **98** 22

book [book] **13** 17

(book of) matches [book′ əv mă′ chəz]
16 28

bookcase [book′ kās] **28** 22, **83** 20

bookstore [book′ stör] **45** 18

boom [boom] **59** 7

booth [booth] **16** 9

boots [boots] **19** 21, **21** 32

bottle [bŏt′ əl] **12** 3, **33** 17

bottle opener [bŏt′ əl ō′ pə nər] **30** 6

bounce [bowns] **97** 11

bow [bō] **98** 7a

bow [bow] **58** 5

bowl [bōl] **13** 23

bowling [bōl′ĭng] **94**

bowling ball [bōl/ĭng böl/] **94** 6
box [bŏks] **13** 12
box seat [bŏks/ sēt/] **99** 11
box spring [bŏks/ sprĭng/] **32** 18
boxer shorts [bŏk/ sər shŏrts/] **22** 2
boxing [bŏk/ sĭng] **94**
boy's frame [boyz/ frām/] **52** 11
bra(ssiere) [brŏ]/[brə zïr/] **22** 13
brace [brās] **36** 9
bracelet [brās/lət] **23** 9
brain [brān] **5** 57
brake [brāk] **50** 26, **52** 17
brake light [brāk/līt/] **50** 29
branch [brănch] **61** 35a
brass [brăs] **98**
bread [brĕd] **14** 12
bread and butter plate
  [brĕd/ ənd bŭt/ ər plāt/] **29** 11
break [brāk] **31** 7
breast [brĕst] **11** 21
bricks [brĭks] **82** 12
bridle path [brīd/ əl păth/] **87** 7
briefcase [brēf/kās/] **21** 37
briefs [brēfs] **22** 12
broccoli [brŏk/ ə lē] **6** 2
broil [broyl] **31** 13
broiler [broy/lər] **30** 33
broken bone [brō/kən bōn/] **40** 15
broom [broom] **35** 7
brother [brŭdh/ ər] **3** 9
brother-in-law [brŭdh/ ər ən lö/] **3** 11
bruise [brooz] **40** 17
brush [brŭsh] **76** 18
brussels sprouts [brŭs/ əl sprowts/] **6** 4
bucket [bŭk/ ət] **35** 15
bucket seat [bŭk/ ət sēt/] **50** 16
buckle [bŭk/ əl] **20** 17
bud [bŭd] **60** 18a
buffet [bə fā/] **29** 29
builder [bĭl/ dər] **82** 5
building number [bĭl/ dĭng nŭm/ bər]
  45 24
bulb [bŭlb] **60** 8a
bull [bool] **67** 34
bulldozer [bool/ dō/ zər] **82** 27
bullet [bool/ ĭt] **48** 26
bulletin board [bool/ ĭ tən börd/] **76** 7
bumper [bŭm/ pər] **33** 5

bun [bŭn] **18** 7
bunch [bŭnch] **8** 1
Bunsen burner [bŭn/ sən bür/ nər]
  78 20
buoy [boo/ ē]/[boy] **58** 16
bureau [byoor/ ō] **32** 9
burn [bürn] **17** 14, **40** 18
burner [bür/ nər] **30** 29
bus [bŭs] **53** 20, **54**
bus driver [bŭs/ drī/ vər] **54** 3
bus stop [bŭs/ stŏp/] **44** 13
busboy [bŭs/ boy/] **16** 3
bushes [boosh/ əz] **61** 41
business workers [biz/ nəs wür/ kərz] **86**
butcher [boo/ chər] **84** 13
butter [bŭt/ ər] **18** 18
buttercup [bŭt/ ər kŭp/] **60** 17
butterfly [bŭt/ ər flī/] **63** 3
buttocks [bŭt/ əks] **4** 15
button [bŭt/ ən] **20** 3, **101** 9
buttonhole [bŭt/ ən hōl/] **101** 8
C-clamp [sē/ klămp/] **36** 2
cab driver [kăb/ drī/ vər] **55** 26
cabbage [kăb/ ĭj] **6** 3
cabin [kăb/ ĭn] **56** 19
cabin cruiser [kăb/ ĭn kroo/ zər] **59** 16
cabinet [kăb/ ə nət] **30** 22
cable [kā/ bəl] **52** 23
cable car [kā/ bəl kär/] **55** 32
cactus [kăk/ təs] **61** 40
calculator [kăl/ kyə lā/ tər] **83** 19,
  100 34
calendar [kăl/ ən dər] **83** 9
calf [kăf] **4** 20, **67** 31
California [kăl/ ə för/ nyə] **72** 5
call card [köl/ kärd/] **47** 6
call number [köl/ nŭm/ bər] **47** 7
call slip [köl/ slĭp/] **47** 12
camel [kăm/ əl] **67** 33
camera [kăm/ ər ə] **100** 8
cameraperson [kăm/ ər ə pür/ sən] **86** 10
camisole [kăm/ ə sōl/] **22** 9
camp stove [kămp/ stōv/] **89** 25
camper [kăm/ pər] **53** 16
campfire [kămp/ fīr/] **89** 31
camping [kăm/ pĭng] **89**
can [kăn] **12** 10
can opener [kăn/ ō/ pə nər] **30** 4

canary [kə nër/ ē] **64** 14
candle [kăn/ dəl] **29** 27
candlestick [kăn/ dəl stĭk/] **29** 28
canister [kăn/ ə stər] **30** 15
canned goods [kănd/ goodz/] **14** 13
cannon [kăn/ ən] **48** 11
canoe [kə noo/] **59** 2
cantaloupe [kăn/ tə lōp/] **9** 36
canyon [kăn/ yən] **88** 3
cap [kăp] **19** 2, **21** 43, **92** 11
capsule [kăp/ səl] **41** 5
car [kär] **54** 9
card catalog [kärd/ kăt/ ə lög] **47** 4
cardigan [kär/ dĭ gən] **21** 26
cardinal [kärd/ nəl] **64** 11
cargo [kär/ gō] **58** 10
cargo area [kär/ gō ër/ ē ə] **57** 12
cargo bay [kär/ gō bā/] **75** 9
cargo door [kär/ gō dör/] **57** 13
Caribbean Sea [kăr/ ə bē/ ən sē/]
  70 20
carpenter [kär/ pən tər] **85** 2
carpenter's rule [kär/ pən tərz rool/]
  36 1
carrot(s) [kăr/ ət(s)] **7** 32
carry [kăr/ ē] **26** 16
carry-on bag [kăr/ ē ŏn băg/] **56** 2
cars [kärz] **50-51**
carton [kär/ tən] **12** 1
cartridge needle [kär/ trĭj nē/ dəl]
  100 19
carve [kärv] **31** 6
cash register [kăsh/ rĕ/ jə stər] **15** 21
cashew(s) [kăsh/ oo(z)] **9** 27
cashier [kă shïr/] **15** 22
Caspian Sea [kăs/ pē ən sē/] **70** 27
casserole dish [kăs/ ə rōl dĭsh/] **30** 14
cassette [kə sĕt/] **100** 26
cassette deck [kə sĕt/ dĕk/] **100** 22
cast [kăst] **39** 5
cat [kăt] **68** 4
catch [kăch] **96** 4
catcher [kăch/ ər] **92** 2, **93** 16
catcher's mask [kăch/ ərz măsk/] **92** 3
catcher's mitt [kăch/ ərz mĭt/] **92** 4
caterpillar [kăt/ ər pĭl/ ər] **63** 1
cattle [kăt/ əl] **81** 20
Caucasus [kö/ kə səs] **71** 45

cauliflower [kŏl′ ə flow′ ər] **6** 1

ceiling [sē′lĭng] **28** 2

ceiling fan [sē ′lĭng făn′] **28** 1

celery [sĕl′ ə rē] **6** 10

cello [chĕl′o] **98** 9

cement [sə mĕnt′] **82** 10

cement mixer [sə mĕnt′ mĭk′ sər]
82 25

cement truck [sə mĕnt′ trŭk′] **49** 13

center [sĕn′ tər] **79** 13, **93** 27

center divider [sĕn′ tər də vī′ dər]
53 18, **82** 24

center fielder [sĕn′ tər fēl′ dər] **93** 2

center lane [sĕn′ tər lān′] **53** 6

centerboard [sĕn′ tər börd′] **59** 6

centipede [sĕn′ tə pēd′] **63** 22

chain [chān] **23** 5, **52** 18

chair [chër] **29** 17

chalk [chök] **76** 10

chalk tray [chök′ trā′] **76** 9

chalkboard [chök′ börd] **76** 5

chandelier [shăn′ də lïr′] **29** 3

change (the sheets) [chānj′ dhə shēts′]
38 13

changing table [chān′ jĭng tā′ bəl] **33** 9

charcoal briquettes
[chär′ köl brĭ kĕts′] **27** 23

chart [chärt] **39** 10

check [chĕk] **15** 27, **16** 14

checked [chĕkt] **24** 18

checkout counter [chĕk′ owt kown′ tər]
15 26

checkout desk [chĕk′ owt dĕsk′] **47** 2

cheerleaders [chïr′ lē′ dərz] **93** 20

cheek [chēk] **4** 35

cherries [chër′ ēz] **9** 19

cherry picker [chër′ ē pĭk′ ər] **82** 18

chest [chĕst] **4** 12

chest of drawers [chĕst′ əv drörz′]
32 30

chestnut(s) [chĕs′ nŭt(s)] **9** 32

chick [chĭk] **64** 22

chicken [chĭk′ ən] **11** 24, **64** 23

child's seat [chīldz′ sēt′] **50** 33

children [chĭl′ drən] **2** 7

chills [chĭlz] **40** 4

chimney [chĭm′ nē] **27** 9

chimpanzee [chĭm păn′ zē] **69** 16

chin [chĭn] **4** 3

china [chī′ nə] **29** 1

china closet [chī′ nə klŏz′ ət] **29** 2

chipmunk [chĭp′ mŭnk] **66** 6

chop [chŏp] **26** 11, **31** 11

chops [chŏps] **10** 9, **10** 15

chorus [kör′ əs] **99** 18

(chrysanthe)mum
[krə săn′ thə məm]/[mŭm] **60** 4

cigarette [sĭg′ ə rĕt′] **16** 31

circle [sür′ kəl] **79** 11

circuit breaker [sür′ kət brā′ kər] **35** 5

circular saw [sür′ kyə lər sö′] **36** 20

circumference [sür kŭm′ fə rəns] **79** 17

citrus fruits [sĭ′ trəs frōots′] **8**

city [sĭt′ ē] **44-45**

clam(s) [klăm(z)] **11** 32

clamp [klămp] **78** 7

clarinet [klăr′ə nĕt′] **98** 16

clasp [klăsp] **23** 17

classroom [klăs′ rōom′] **76**

claw [klö] **62** 13a, **68** 2a

clean [klēn] **24** 6, **26** 2

cleanser [klĕn′ zər] **35** 9

clear [klïr] **17** 6

cliff [klĭf] **89** 21

clip-on earring [klĭp′ ŏn ïr′ ĭng] **23** 15

clock [klŏk] **76** 2

close (v) [klōz] **77** 5

closed [klōzd] **24** 16

closet [klŏz′ ət] **32** 3

cloth diaper [klöth′ dī′ pər] **33** 13

clothes [klōz] **19-24**

clothesline [klōz′ līn′] **35** 19

clothespins [klōz′ pĭnz′] **35** 20

cloudy [klow′ dē] **25** 2

clove [klōv] **7** 25a

cloverleaf [klō′ vər lēf′] **53** 4

clubs [klŭbz] **95** 5

clutch [klŭch] **50** 25

coach [kōch] **93** 21

coal [kōl] **80** 7

coal mine [kōl′ mīn′] **80** 6

coaster [kō′ stər] **16** 27

coat [kōt] **19** 24, **42** 13

cob [kŏb] **6** 12a

cobra [kō′ brə] **65** 11

cockpit [kŏk′ pĭt′] **56** 13

cockroach [kŏk′ rōch′] **63** 9

cocktail lounge [kŏk′ tāl lownj′] **16**

cocktail waitress [kŏk′ tāl wā′ trəs]
16 32

cocoon [kə kōon′] **63** 2

coconut [kō′ kə nŭt′] **8** 3

coffee [kö′ fē] **18** 35

coffeemaker [kö′ fē mā′ kər] **30** 31

coffeepot [kö′ fē pŏt′] **29** 18

coffee table [kö′ fē tā′ bəl] **28** 26

coins [koynz] **13** 26

colander [kŏl′ ən dər] **30** 7

cold [kōld] **25** 10, **40** 11

cold water faucet [kōld′ wŏ tər fö′ sət]
34 18

collar [kŏl′ ər] **20** 20

colonial-style house
[kə lō′ nē əl stīl hows′] **27**

Colorado [kŏl′ ə rŏd′ ō] **72** 6

column [kŏl′ əm] **50** 13

comb [kōm] **32** 6

combine (n) [kŏm′ bīn] **81** 17

comet [kŏm′ ət] **74** 2

comforter [kŭm′ fər tər] **32** 22

command module [kə mănd′ mŏj′ ōol]
75 8

communication satellite
[kə myōo′ nə kā shən săt′ ə līt] **75** 2

commuter [kə myōo′ tər] **55** 17

commuter train [kə myōo′ tər trān′]
55 14

compact disc (CD)
[kŏm′ păkt dĭsk′]/[sē′ dē′] **100** 27

compact disc player
[kŏm′ păkt dĭsk′ plā′ ər] **100** 28

computer [kəm pyōo′ tər] **76** 8, **83**
16, **100**

computer programmer
[kəm pyōo′ tər prō′ grăm ər] **86** 16

conductor [kən dŭk′ tər] **54** 7, **99** 8

cone [kōn] **61** 34b, **79** 28, **82** 19

conga [kŏng′ gə] **98** 20

Congo River [kŏng′ gō rĭv′ ər] **71** 62

Connecticut [kə nĕ′ tĭ kət] **72** 7

constellation [kŏn′ stə lā′ shən] **74** 3

construction [kən strŭk′ shən] **82**

(construction) boots
[kən strŭk′ shən bōots′] **21** 32

construction site [kən strŭk′shən sīt′] **82**

construction worker
[kən strŭk′shən wür′kər] **82** 14

container [kən tā′nər] **12** 2, **58** 7

(container)ship [kən tā′nər shĭp′] **58** 9

containers [kən tā′nərz] **12**

continents [kŏn′tə nənts] **70**

control tower [kən trōl′tow′ər] **57** 20

conveyor belt [kən vā′ər bĕlt] **15** 23,
56 12

cook (n) [ko͝ok] **16** 1

cook (v) [ko͝ok] **17** 4

cookie [ko͝ok′ē] **18** 22

cool [ko͞ol] **25** 9

cooler [ko͞o′lər] **91** 41

cooling tower [ko͞o′lĭng tow′ər] **80** 16

copilot [kō′pī lət] **56** 16

cord [körd] **32** 26a, **54** 1

(corduroy) pants [kör′də roy pănts′]
21 27

core [kör] **8** 2b, **80** 14

cork [körk] **16** 18

corkscrew [körk′skro͞o′] **16** 17

corn [körn] **6** 12, **60** 24

corner [kör′nər] **44** 3

corral [kə răl′] **81** 24

cosmetics [kŏz mĕt′ĭks] **23**

cotton balls [kŏt′ən bölz′] **39** 23

cotton swab [kŏt′ən swŏb′] **33** 10

counter [kown′tər] **30** 27

court [kört] **43**, **94** 13

court officer [kört′ö′fə sər] **43** 19

court reporter [kört′rə pör′tər] **43** 14

cousin [kŭz′ən] **3** 7

cow [kow] **67** 32

cowboy [kow′boy′] **81** 21

cowgirl [kow′gürl′] **81** 22

crab(s) [krăb(z)] **11** 36, **62** 9

cradle [krā′dəl] **33** 26

cranberries [krăn′bĕr′ēz] **8** 13

crane [krān] **58** 6

creamer [krē′mər] **29** 24

crew [kro͞o] **75** 12

(crewneck) sweater
[kro͞o′nĕk swĕt′ər] **19** 7

crib [krĭb] **33** 4

criket [krĭk′ət] **63** 5

crime [krīm] **43**

crochet [krō shā′] **101** 28

crochet hook [krō′shā′ho͝ok′] **101** 29

crocus [krō′kəs] **60** 9

cross-country skiing
[krös′kŭn trē skē′ĭng] **94**

crosswalk [krös′wök′] **44** 4

crow [krō] **64** 3

crutch [krŭch] **39** 7

cube [kyo͞ob] **79** 27

cubicle [kyo͞o′bə kəl] **83** 5

cucumber(s) [kyo͞o′kŭm bər(z)] **7** 20

cuff links [kŭf′lĭnks′] **23** 12

cup [kŭp] **13** 19, **29** 20

curb [kürb] **45** 26

curtain [kür′tən] **32** 10, **99** 1

curtain rings [kür′tən rĭngz′] **34** 2

curtain rod [kür′tən rŏd′] **34** 1

curve [kürv] **79** 3

cushion [ko͝osh′ən] **28** 24

customer [kŭs′tə mər] **15** 17

cut (v) [kŭt] **31** 9

cut (n) [kŭt] **40** 16

cutting board [kŭt′ĭng börd′] **30** 26

cylinder [sĭl′ĭn dər] **79** 26

cymbals [sĭm′bəlz] **98** 18

daffodil [dăf′ə dĭl] **60** 8

dairy cow [dër′ē kow′] **81** 11

dairy farm [dër′ē färm′] **81**

dairy products [dër′ē prŏd′ŭkts] **14** 4

daisy [dā′zē] **60** 5

dam [dăm] **80** 18

dance [dăns] **99**

dancer [dăn′sər] **99** 3

dark [därk] **24** 10

dashboard [dăsh′börd′] **50** 19

date [dāt] **9** 23

daughter [dö′tər] **3** 15

deck [dĕk] **27** 5, **58** 22

deer [dïr] **67** 26

defendant [də fĕn′dənt] **43** 23

defense attorney [də fĕns′ə tür′nē]
43 22

Delaware [dĕl′ə wăr′] **72** 8

deli counter [dĕl′ē kown′tər] **14** 1

delivery boy [də lĭv′ə rē boy′] **85** 10

delivery person [də lĭv′ə rē pür′sən]
49 10

dental care [dĕn′təl kër′] **39**

dentist [dĕn′tĭst] **39** 17

department store [də pärt′mənt stör′]
44 5

depth [dĕpth] **79** 33

derrick [dĕr′ĭk] **80** 2

deserts [dĕz′ərts] **71**

desk [dĕsk] **28** 14, **76** 16, **83** 13

detective [də tĕk′tĭv] **43** 2

diagonal [dī ăg′ə nəl] **79** 20

diameter [dī ăm′ə tər] **79** 12

dictionary [dĭk′shə nër′ē] **47** 24

diesel fuel [dē′zəl fyo͞o′əl] **80** 34

dig [dĭg] **26** 3

dime [dīm] **13** 29

dinghy [dĭng′ē] **59** 18

dining room [dī′nĭng ro͞om′] **29**

dipstick [dĭp′stĭk′] **51** 58

dirt bike [dürt′bīk′] **52** 8

disc jockey (DJ) [dĭsk′jŏk′ē]/[dē′jā]
86 9

dirty [dür′tē] **24** 5

dish drainer [dĭsh′drā′nər] **30** 2

dish towel [dĭsh′tow′əl] **30** 18

dishwasher [dĭsh′wŏsh′ər] **30** 1

dishwashing liquid
[dĭsh′wŏsh ĭng lĭ′kwĭd] **30** 10

disposable diaper
[dīs pō′zə bəl dī′pər] **33** 12

dissection kit [dĭ sĕk′shən kĭt′] **78** 33

dive [dīv] **97** 14

dock [dŏk] **58** 28

doctor [dŏk′tər] **39** 11

dogs [dögz] **69**

dogwood [dög′wo͝od′] **61** 28

doll [dŏl] **33** 28

doll house [dŏl′hows′] **33** 25

dollar bills [dŏl′ər bĭlz′] **13** 25

dolly [dŏl′ē] **56** 6

dolphin [dŏl′fĭn] **68** 13

donkey [dŏng′kē] **67** 23

door handle [dör′hăn′dəl] **50** 4

door lock [dör′lŏk′] **50** 1

doorman [dör′mən] **85** 11

down [down] **103** 3

down vest [down′vĕst′] **19** 12

dragonfly [drăg′ən flī′] **63** 4

drain [drān] **34** 9

drainpipe [drān′pīp′] **27** 18

drapes [drāps] **28** 23

draw [drö] **77** 11

drawer [drör] **47** 5

dress [drĕs] **20** 22

dried fruits [drīd′ frōōts′] **9**

drill [drĭl] **39** 15

drink [drĭngk] **17** 2

drive [drīv] **97** 15

driveway [drīv′ wā′] **27** 1

drugstore [drŭg′ stör′] **45** 22

drum [drŭm] **98** 19

drummer [drŭm′ ər] **99** 27

drumsticks [drŭm′ stĭks′] **98** 19a

dry [drī] **25** 14, **38** 9

dryer [drī′ər] **35** 24

duck [dŭk] **11** 25, **64** 25

(duck) pond [dŭk′ pŏnd′] **87** 8

dugout [dŭg′ owt′] **93** 13

dump truck [dŭmp′ trŭk′] **49** 14

dust [dŭst] **38** 15

dustpan [dŭst′ păn′] **35** 8

eagle [ē′ gəl] **64** 5

ear [ïr] **4** 34

(ear of) corn [ïr′ əv körn′] **6** 12

earmuffs [ïr′ mŭfs′] **19** 10

earrings [ïr′ ĭngz] **23** 1

Earth [ürth] **74** 8, **13**

east [ēst] **71** 73

East China Sea [ēst′ chī′ nə sē′]
   70 38

eat [ēt] **17** 1

eel [ēl] **65** 4

egg [ĕg] **18** 32, **64** 13

egg roll [ĕg′ rōl′] **18** 25

eggplant [ĕg′ plănt′] **7** 21

elbow [ĕl′ bō] **4** 8

electric drill [ĭ lĕk′ trĭk drĭl′] **37** 43

electric guitar [ĭ lĕk′ trĭk gĭ tär′]
   99 26

electric generator
   [ĭ lĕk′ trĭk gĕn′ ə rā tər] **80** 21

electrical tape [ĭ lĕk′ trĭ kəl tāp′]
   37 34

electrician [ĭ lĕk trĭ′ shən] **85** 6

electricity [ĭ lĕk trĭs′ ĭ tē] **80** 32

electronics [ĭ lĕk trŏn′ ĭks] **100**

elephant [ĕl′ ə fənt] **66** 17

elevator [ĕl′ ə vā′ tər] **45** 17, **80** 9

elm [ĕlm] **61** 36

embroidery [ĕm broi′ də rē] **101** 27

emergency brake [ĭ mür′ jən sē brāk′]
   50 15

emery board [ĕm′ ə rē börd′] **23** 24

encyclopedia [ĕn sī′ klə pē′ dē ə] **47** 25

end table [ĕnd′ tā′ bəl] **28** 29

end zone [ĕnd′ zōn′] **93** 23

energy [ĕn′ ər jē] **80**

engagement ring [ĕn gāj′ mənt rĭng′]
   23 3

engine [ĕn′ jən] **51, 52** 32

engineer [ĕn′ jə nïr′] **55** 15

enter [ĕn′ tər] **77** 14

entrance ramp [ĕn′ trəns rămp′] **53** 21

envelope [ĕn′ və lōp′] **46** 16, **83** 31

equator [ĭ kwā′ tər] **71** 70

erase [ĭ rās′] **77** 3

eraser [ĭ rā′ sər] **76** 11

escarole [ĕs′ kə rōl′] **6** 7

esophagus [ĭ sŏf′ ə gəs] **5** 61

eucalyptus [yōō′ kə lĭp′ təs] **61** 27

Europe [yŏŏr′ əp] **70** 3

examining table [ĭg zăm′ ə nĭng tā′ bəl]
   39 6

exhaust pipe [ĭg zöst′ pīp′] **52** 33

exit ramp [ĕg′ zĭt rămp′] **53** 2

exit sign [ĕg′ zĭt sīn′] **53** 24

Express Mail (package)
   [ĭk sprĕs′ māl păk′ ĭj] **46** 23

extension cord [ĭk stĕn′ shən körd′]
   36 5

eye [ī] **5**

eye drops [ī′ drŏps′] **41** 10

eye shadow [ī′ shă′ dō] **23** 30

eyebrow [ī′ brow′] **5** 44

eyebrow pencil [ī′ brow pĕn′ səl]
   23 26

eyelashes [ī′ lăsh′ əz] **5** 46

eyelid [ī′ lĭd′] **5** 45

eyeliner [ī′ lī′ nər] **23** 33

fabric softener [făb′ rĭk sö′ fə nər]
   35 27

face [fās] **4** 1

face guard [fās′ gärd′] **92** 15

factory work [făk′ tə rē würk′] **85**

fairway [fĕr′ wā′] **95** 12

fall [föl] **96** 7

Fall [föl] **26**

family [făm′ ə lē] **3**

family restaurant [făm′ ə lē rĕs′ tər ənt]
   16

fan belt [făn′ bĕlt′] **51** 53

fare [fĕr] **55** 21

fare box [fĕr′ bŏks′] **54** 5

farmhouse [färm′ hows′] **81** 3

farmer [fär′ mər] **81** 7

farming [fär′ mĭng] **81**

fashion designer [făsh′ ən də zī′ nər]
   86 6

father [fŏdh′ ər] **3** 5

faucet [fö′ sĭt] **34** 17, 18

fawn [fön] **67** 27

feather [fĕdh′ ər] **64** 7a

feather duster [fĕdh′ ər dŭs′ tər] **35** 2

fence [fĕns] **81** 9

fender [fĕn′ dər] **52** 10

ferry [fĕr′ ē] **58** 17

fever [fē′ vər] **40** 2

field [fēld] **81** 16

fields and courses [fēldz′ ənd kör′ səz]
   95

fig [fĭg] **9** 21

fighter plane [fī′ tər plān′] **48** 1

file cabinet [fīl′ kăb′ ə nət] **83** 21

file clerk [fīl′ klürk′] **83** 23

file folder [fīl′ fōl′ dər] **83** 22

filet [fĭ lā′] **11** 28

fill [fĭl] **26** 9

film [fĭlm] **100** 10, **100** 17

filter paper [fĭl′ tər pā′ pər] **78** 16

fin [fĭn] **65** 3b

finger [fĭng′ gər] **4** 25

fingernail [fĭng′ gər nāl′] **4** 23

fingerprints [fĭng′ gər prĭnts′] **43** 24

finish line [fĭn′ ĭsh līn′] **95** 21

fire [fīr] **28** 9, **42** 5

fire engine [fīr′ ĕn′ jən] **42** 2

fire escape [fīr′ ə skāp′] **42** 4

fire extinguisher
   [fīr′ ĭk stĭng′ gwĭ shər] **42** 11

fire fighter [fīr′ fī′ tər] **42** 10

fire hydrant [fīr′ hī′ drənt] **42** 9

fire truck [fīr′ trŭk′] **42** 3

firefighting [fīr′ fī′ tĭng] **42**

firefly [fīr′ flī′] **63** 17

fireplace [fīr′ plās′] **28** 8

first baseman [fürst′ bās′ mən] **93** 8

first quarter [fürst′ kwör′ tər] **74** 23

fish [fĭsh] **11** 26, **65**

fisherman [fĭsh′ ər mən] **58** 2

fishing [fĭsh′ ĭng] **88**

fishing boat [fĭsh′ ĭng bōt′] **58** 1

fishing line [fĭsh′ ĭng līn′] **88** 8

fishing net [fĭsh′ ĭng nĕt′] **88** 9

fishing rod [fĭsh′ ĭng rŏd′] **88** 7

flag [flăg] **76** 1, **82** 20, **95** 9

flame [flām] **29** 26, **78** 21

flamingo [flə mĭng′ gō] **64** 29

flanker [flăng′ kər] **93** 31

flannel shirt [flăn′ əl shürt′] **19** 3

flare [flër] **51** 41

flash [flăsh] **100** 7

flashlight [flăsh′ līt′] **35** 3

flask [flăsk] **78** 2

(flat) sheet [flăt′ shēt′] **32** 19

flatbed [flăt′ bĕd′] **49** 18

flight attendant [flīt′ ə tĕn′ dənt] **56** 20

flight deck [flīt′ dĕk′] **75** 10

flight engineer [flīt′ ĕn jə nïr′] **56** 17

flipper [flĭp′ ər] **68** 12a

flippers [flĭp′ ərz] **91** 36

floor [flör] **32** 29

Florida [flör′ ə də] **72** 9

florist [flör′ ĭst] **84** 11

flounder [flown′ dər] **65** 7

flowers [flow′ ərz] **60**

flute [flōōt] **99** 13

fly [flī] **63** 18

flying mammal [flī′ ĭng mă′ məlz] **66**

foal [fōl] **67** 22

foggy [fög′ ē] **25** 12

fold [fōld] **38** 1

food [fōōd] **6-18**

foot [fŏŏt] **5**

football [fŏŏt′ böl′] **92, 92** 13

football field [fŏŏt′ böl fēld′] **93**

forceps [för′ səps] **78** 28

forearm [för′ ärm′] **4** 9

forehead [för′ hĕd′] **4** 32

forelegs [för′ lĕgz′] **66** 3d

foreman [för′ mən] **85** 13

fork [förk] **29** 12

forklift [förk′ lĭft′] **58** 4

foul line [fowl′ līn′] **93** 9

foundation [fown dā′ shən] **82** 11

four-door hatchback [för′ dör hăch′ băk] **51**

fox [fŏks] **68** 6

fractions [frăk′ shənz] **79**

frame [frām] **28** 4

frame backpack [frām′ băk′ păk] **89** 28

freezer [frē′ zər] **14** 3, **30** 20

freezing [frē′ zĭng] **25** 11

french fries [frĕnch′ frīz′] **18** 28

French horn [frĕnch′ hörn′] **98** 26

fried chicken [frīd′ chĭk′ ən] **18** 29

Frisbee™ [frĭz′ bē] **90** 13

frog [frŏg] **65** 17

from [frŭm] **103** 10

front bumper [frŭnt′ bŭm′ pər] **51** 51

frozen foods [frō′zən fōōdz′] **14** 2

fruit and vegetable market [frōōt′ ənd vĕj′ tə bəl mär′ kət] **45** 28

fruit tree [frōōt′ trē′] **81** 2

fruits [frōōts] **8**

fry [frī] **31** 15

frying pan [frī′ ĭng păn′] **30** 5

fuel truck [fyōō′ əl trŭk′] **49** 3

full moon [fŏŏl′ mōōn′] **74** 24

full slip [fŏŏl′ slĭp′] **22** 10

fullback [fŏŏl′ băk′] **93** 34

funnel [fŭn′ əl] **78** 17

fuselage [fyōō′ sə lŏj′] **57** 14

galaxy [găl′ək sē] **74** 1

Ganges River [găn′ jēz rĭv′ər] **71** 67

gangway [găng′ wā′] **58** 20

garage [gə röj′] **27** 2

garbage can [gär′ bĭj kăn′] **35** 31

garbage truck [gär′ bĭj trŭk′] **49** 6

garden hose [gär′ dən hōs′] **27** 14

gardenia [gär dēn′ yə] **60** 14

gardener [gärd′ nər] **85** 3

garlic [gär′ lĭk] **7** 25

garment bag [gär′ mənt băg′] **56** 1

garter belt [gär′ tər bĕlt′] **22** 14

(garter) snake [gär′ tər snāk′] **65** 9

gas gauge [găs′ gāj′] **50** 9

gas pump [găs′ pŭmp′] **53** 14

gas tank [găs′ tănk′] **50** 34

gas(oline) [găs′ ə lēn′] **80** 28

(gauze) bandage [göz′ băn′ dĭj] **39** 24

gauze pads [göz′ pădz′] **39** 25

gavel [găv′ əl] **43** 12

gear [gïr] **89** 27

gear changer [gïr′ chān′ jər] **52** 22

gearshift [gïr′ shĭft′] **50** 17

geometrical figures [jē′ ə mĕ′ trĭ kəl fĭg′ yərz] **79**

Georgia [jör′ jə] **72** 10

geyser [gī′ zər] **80** 5

gibbon [gĭb′ ən] **69** 15

gill .[gĭl] **65** 3c

giraffe [jə răf′] **67** 29

girdle [gür′ dəl] **22** 15

girl [gürl] **2** 9

girl's frame [gürlz′ frām′] **52** 3

give [gĭv] **17** 9

glass [glăs] **12** 20

glasses [glăs′ əz] **21** 44

glider [glī′ dər] **57** 4

globe [glōb] **47** 19

glove [glŭv] **92** 12, **94** 11, **94** 15

glove compartment [glŭv′ kəm pärt′ mənt] **50** 20

gloves [glŭvz] **19** 1

glue [glōō] **37** 33, **76** 17

goal [gōl] **92** 25

goalie [gōl′ ē] **92** 24

goalpost [gōl′ pōst′] **93** 35

goat [gōt] **67** 28

Gobi Desert [gō′ bē dĕz′ ərt] **71** 54

golf [gŏlf] **94**

golf bag [gŏlf′ băg′] **95** 7

golf ball [gŏlf′ böl′] **94** 7

golf cart [gŏlf′ kärt′] **95** 8

golf course [gŏlf′ körs′] **95**

golfer [gŏl′ fər] **94** 10

goose [gōōs] **64** 26

gooseberries [gōōs′ bër′ ēz] **8** 11

gopher [gō′ fər] **66** 8

gorilla [gə rĭl′ ə] **69** 17

graduated cylinder [grăj′ ōō ā tĭd sĭl′ ən dər] **78** 25

grains [grānz] **60**

granddaughter [grănd′ dö′ tər] **2** 11

grandfather [grănd′ fö′ dhər] **3** 2

grandmother [grănd′ mŭ′ dhər] **3** 1

grandparents [grănd păr′ ənts] **2** 10

grandson [grănd′ sŭn′] **2** 12

grapefruit [grăp′ frōōt′] **8** 7

grapes [grāps] **8** 1

graph paper [grăf′ pā′ pər] **78** 11

grass [grăs] **27** 15

grasses [grăs′ əz] **60**

grasshopper [grăs′ hŏp′ ər] **63** 6

grate [grāt] **31** 2

Great Sandy Desert
[grāt′ săn′ dē dĕz′ ərt] **71** 55

green [grēn] **95** 10

greengrocer [grēn′ grō′ sər] **84** 7

grill [grĭl] **27** 22, **88** 12

grizzly bear [grĭz′ lē bër′] **69** 23

groceries [grō′ sə rēz] **15** 24

ground beef [grownd′ bēf′] **10** 2

grounding plug [grown′ dĭng plŭg′]
36 7

guitar [gĭ tär′] **98** 11

Gulf of Alaska [gŭlf′ əv ə lăs′kə]
70 17

Gulf of Guinea [gŭlf′ əv gĭn′ ē] **70** 25

Gulf of Mexico [gŭlf′ əv mĕk sə kō′]
70 19

gulfs [gŭlfs] **70**

gun [gŭn] **43** 7

gun turret [gŭn′ tür′ ət] **48** 12

gutter [gŭt′ ər] **27** 10, **94** 3

gymnast [jĭm′ nəst] **94** 23

gymnastics [jĭm năs′ tĭks] **94**

hacksaw [hăk′ sö′] **36** 18

hair [hër] **4** 30

hair dryer [hër′ drī′ ər] **34** 26

hairbrush [hër′ brŭsh′] **32** 7

hairdresser [hër′ drĕs′ ər] **84** 10

half (1/2) [hăf] **79** 30

half slip [hăf′ slĭp′] **22** 8

halfback [hăf′ băk′] **93** 33

hall [höl] **76** 12

ham [hăm] **10** 12

hamburger [hăm′bür′ gər] **18** 9

hammer [hăm′ ər] **36** 13

hammock [hăm′ ək] **27** 11

hamper [hăm′ pər] **34** 28

hand [hănd] **4**

hand brake [hănd′ brāk′] **52** 24

hand grenade [hănd′ grə nād′] **48** 29

hand towel [hănd′ tow′ əl] **34** 23

hand truck [hănd′ trŭk′] **87** 4

handball [hănd′ böl′] **94**, **94** 12

handcuffs [hănd′ kŭfs′] **43** 4

handicrafts [hăn′ dē krăfts′] **101**

handlebars [hăn′ dəl bärz′] **52** 2

hang [hăng] **38** 6

hang glider [hăng′ glī′ dər] **57** 6

hangar [hăng′ ər] **57** 17

hanger [hăng′ ər] **32** 2

hard hat [härd′ hăt′] **21** 28, **82** 4

harmonica [här mŏn′ ə kə] **98** 30

harness [här′ nəs] **89** 22

harp [härp] **98** 6

hat [hăt] **19** 18

hatchback [hăch′ băk′] **51** 43

hatchet [hăch′ ət] **36** 17

Hawaii [hə wö′ ē] **72** 11

hawk [hök] **64** 7

hay [hā] **81** 13

hazelnut(s) [hā′ zəl nŭt(s)′] **9** 30

head [hĕd] **4**, **37** 42a

(head of) cauliflower
[hĕd′ əv köl ə flow′ ər] **6** 1

head protector [hĕd prə tĕk′ tər] **94** 14

headache [hĕd′ āk′] **40** 6

headboard [hĕd′ börd′] **32** 14

headlights [hĕd′ līts′] **51** 48

headphones [hĕd′ fōnz′] **100** 29

headrest [hĕd′ rĕst′] **50** 35

headset [hĕd′ sĕt′] **83** 2

heart [härt] **5** 64

heat [hēt] **80** 27

heating pad [hē′ tĭng păd′] **41** 3

hedge clippers [hĕj′ klĭp′ ərz] **27** 29

heel [hēl] **5** 50, **20** 5

heels [hēlz] **20** 25

height [hīt] **79** 34

helicopter [hĕl′ə kŏp′ tər] **57** 2

helmet [hĕl′ mət] **42** 12, **52** 7, **92** 14

hem [hĕm] **101** 11

hem binding [hĕm′ bīn′ dĭng] **101** 12

herb(s) [ürb(z)] **6** 9

(herd of) cattle [hürd′ əv kăt′ əl] **81** 20

high [hī] **24** 11

high blood pressure [hī′ blŭd prĕsh′ ər]
40 10

high chair [hī′ chër′] **16** 8

high heels [hī′ hēlz′] **20** 25

highway travel [hī′ wā trăv′ əl] **53**

hikers [hī′ kərz] **88** 2

hiking boots [hī′ kĭng bōōts′] **19** 9

hill [hĭl] **88** 4

Himalayas [hĭm′ ə lā′ əz] **70** 47

hind legs [hīnd′ lĕgz′] **66** 3b

hip [hĭp] **4** 16

hippopotamus [hĭp′ ə pŏt′ ə məs]
66 14

hit [hĭt] **96** 1

hitchhiker [hĭch′ hī′ kər] **53** 9

hockey stick [hŏk′ ē stĭk′] **92** 18

hog [hög] **66** 30

hold [hōld] **17** 12, **58** 8

hole [hōl] **94** 8

holly [hŏl′ ē] **61** 37

holster [hōl′ stər] **43** 8

home plate [hōm′ plāt′] **93** 15

honeydew melon
[hŭn′ ē dōō mĕl′ ən] **9** 35

hood [hōōd] **51** 47

hoof [hōōf] **66** 35b

hoofed mammals [hōōft′ măm′ əlz] **66**

hook [hōōk] **32** 1, **36** 16

hook and eye [hōōk′ ənd ī′] **101** 14

horn [hörn] **50** 12, **52** 5, **66** 16a

horse [hörs] **66** 21

horse racing [hörs′ rā′ sĭng] **94**

horse-drawn carriage
[hörs′ drön kăr′ ĭj] **54** 33

horseback rider [hörs′ băk rī′ dər]
87 6

horses [hörs′ əz] **81** 23

hose [hōz] **42** 8, **50** 57

hot [hŏt] **25** 7

hot air balloon [hŏt′ ër bə lōōn′] **57** 1

hot dog [hŏt′ dög′] **18** 2

hot water faucet [hŏt′ wŏt ər fö′ sət]
34 17

house plants [hows′ plănts′] **60** 39

household items [hows′ hōld ī′ təmz]
15 15

household services
[hows′ hōld sür′ və səz] **85**

housekeeper [hows′ kē′ pər] **85** 8

houses [how′ zəz] **27**

housework [hows′ würk′] **38**

Huang River [hwöng′ riv′ər] **71** 68

hubcap [hŭb′ kăp′] **50** 36

Hudson Bay [hŭd/ sən bā/] **70** 18

human body [hyōō/ mən bŏd/ ē] **4**

hummingbird [hŭm/ ĭng bürd/] **64** 2

hump [hŭmp] **67** 33a

husband [hŭz/ bənd] **2** 3, **3** 12

hyacinth [hī/ ə sĭnth] **60** 10

hyena [hī ē/ nə] **68** 30

hypotenuse [hī pŏt/ ə nōōs/] **79** 24

ice cream cone [īs/ krēm cōn/] **18** 36

ice hockey [īs/ hŏk/ ē] **92**

ice pack [īs/ păk/] **41** 4

ice skates [īs/ skāts/] **19** 15

ice skating [īs/ skā/ tĭng] **94**

ice tray [īs/ trā/] **30** 21

icy [ī/ sē] **25** 16

Idaho [ī/ də hō/] **72** 12

ignition [ĭg nĭsh/ ən] **50** 14

iguana [ĭ gwŏ/ nə] **65** 13

Illinois [ĭl/ ə noy/] **72** 13

in [ĭn] **102** 7

in front of [ĭn frŭnt/ əv] **102** 6

in-box [ĭn/ bŏks] **83** 12

(index) finger [ĭn/ dĕks fĭng/ gər] **4** 25

Indian Ocean [ĭn/ dē ən ō/ shən/] **70** 13

Indiana [ĭn/ dē ăn/ ə] **72** 14

individual sports
[ĭn/ də vĭj/ ōō əl spörts/] **94**

infection [ĭn fĕk/ shən] **40** 14

inflatable raft [ĭn flā/ tə bəl răft/] **59** 20

information desk
[ĭn/ fər mā/ shən dĕsk/] **47** 22

injection [ĭn jĕk/ shən] **41** 8

injuries [ĭn/ jə rēz] **40**

insect bite [ĭn/ sĕkt bīt/] **40** 3

insects [ĭn/ sĕkts] **63**

instep [ĭn/ stĕp/] **5** 51

instruments [ĭn/ strə mənts]
39 13, **56** 14, **98**

internal organs [ĭn tür/ nəl ör/ gənz] **5**

intersection [ĭn/ tər sĕk/ shən] **44** 11

interstate highway
[ĭn/ tər stāt hī/ wā] **53** 1

intestines [ĭn tĕs/ tənz] **5** 67

into [ĭn/ tōō] **103** 12

Iowa [ī/ ə wə] **72** 15

iris [ī/ rəs] **5** 47, **60** 11

iron (n) [ī/ ərn] **35** 12

iron (v) [ī/ ərn] **38** 11

ironing board [ī/ ər nĭng börd/] **35** 13

jack [jăk] **32** 26b, **50** 38

jacket [jăk/ ət] **19** 17, **21** 33

jackhammer [jăk/ hăm/ər] **82** 22

jail [jāl] **43** 1

janitor [jăn/ə tər] **85** 9

jar [jär] **12** 9

jaw [jö] **4** 38

jeans [jēnz] **19** 6

jeep [jēp] **48** 9

jelly [jĕl/ ē] **18** 31

jellyfish [jĕl/ ē fĭsh/] **62** 12

jet engine [jĕt/ ĕn/ jən] **57** 11

jet fuel [jĕt/ fyōō/ əl] **80** 31

(jet) plane [jĕt/ plān/] **57** 18

jeweller [jōō/ ə lər] **84** 12

jewelry [jōō/ əl rē] **23**

jewelry box [jōō/ əl rē bŏks/] **32** 4

jigsaw [jĭg/ sö] **36** 3

jockey [jŏk/ ē] **94** 21

jogging path [jŏg/ ĭng păth/] **87** 9

judge [jŭj] **43** 10

jukebox [jōōk/ bŏks/] **16** 12

jump [jŭmp] **96** 8

jungle gym [jŭng/ əl jĭm/] **87** 17

Jupiter [jōō/ pə tər] **74** 15

jury [jŏŏr/ ē] **43** 21

jury box [joor/ ē bŏks/] **43** 20

kangaroo [kăng/ gə rōō/] **66** 3

Kansas [kăn/ zəs] **72** 16

Kara Sea [kär/ ə sē/] **70** 31

kayak [kī/ ăk] **59** 17

Kentucky [kĕn tŭk/ ē] **72** 17

ketchup [kĕch/ əp] **16** 4

kettledrum [kĕt/ əl drŭm/] **98** 21

keyboard [kē/ börd/] **98** 1a, **100** 33

keyboard player [kē/ börd plā/ ər] **99** 22

kickstand [kĭk/ stănd/] **52** 9

kidney [kĭd/ nē] **5** 70

kidney bean(s) [kĭd/ nē bēn(z)/] **6** 13

kitchen [kĭch/ ən] **30**

kite [kīt] **91** 22

kitten [kĭt/ ən] **68** 5

knee [nē] **4** 19

knee socks [nē/ sŏks/] **22** 16

knife [nīf] **29** 15

knitting [nĭt/ ĭng] **101** 22

knitting needle [nĭt/ ĭng nē/ dəl] **101** 25

knuckle [nŭk/ əl] **4** 22

koala [kō ŏl/ ə] **66** 1

label [lā/ bəl] **46** 21

lacrosse [lə krös/] **92**

lacrosse stick [lə krös/ stĭk/] **92** 16

ladder [lăd/ ər] **42** 1, **82** 8

ladybug [lā/ dē bŭg/] **63** 14

lamb [lăm] **10** 13, **67** 24

lamp [lămp] **28** 28

lampshade [lămp/ shād/] **28** 27

landing gear [lăn/ dĭng gĭr/] **57** 15

lane [lān] **94** 4

lantern [lăn/ tərn] **88** 29

lapel [lə pĕl/] **20** 1

Laptev Sea [lăp/ tĕv sē/] **70** 33

last quarter [lăst/ kwör/ tər] **74** 25

launchpad [lönch/ păd/] **75** 15

laundry [lön/ drē] **35** 28

laundry basket [lön/ drē băs/ kət] **35** 29

laundry detergent [lön/ drē də tür/ jənt]
35 25

lawn mower [lön/ mō/ ər] **27** 12

lead guitarist [lēd/ gĭ tär/ ĭst] **99** 25

leaf [lēf] **60** 36a

leave [lēv] **77** 13

left fielder [lĕft/ fēl/ dər] **93** 1

left guard [lĕft/ gärd/] **93** 26

left lane [lĕft/ lān/] **53** 5

left tackle [lĕft/ tăk/ əl] **93** 25

leg [lĕg] **4** 17, **10** 14, **11** 20

(legal) pad [lē/ gəl păd/] **83** 26

lemon [lĕm/ ən] **8** 9

Lena River [lē/ nə rĭv/ ər] **71** 66

length [lĕngth] **79** 36

lens [lĕnz] **100** 6

leopard [lĕp/ ərd] **68** 1

letter [lĕt/ ər] **46** 7

letter carrier [lĕt/ ər kăr/ yər] **46** 3

lettuce [lĕt/ əs] **6** 6

level [lĕv/ əl] **82** 3

librarian [lī brĕr/ ē ən] **47** 23

library card [lī/ brĕr ē kärd/] **47** 3

library clerk [lī/ brĕr ē klürk/] **47** 1

license plate [lī/ səns plāt/] **50** 28

lid [lĭd] **30** 9

life jacket [līf/ jăk/ ət] **59** 1

life preserver [līf/ prə zür/ vər] **90** 9

lifeboat [līf/ bōt/] **58** 19, **90** 10

lifeguard [līf/ gärd/] **90** 6

lifeguard chair [līf/ gärd chër/] **90** 8

light (v) [līt] **17** 13

light (adj) [līt] **24** 9

light switch [līt/ swĭch/] **32** 25

lightbulb [līt/ bŭlb/] **35** 22

lighter [lī/ tər] **16** 30

lighthouse [līt/ hows/] **58** 14

lily [lĭl/ ē] **60** 3

lima bean(s) [lī/ mə bēn(z)/] **6** 16

lime [līm] **8** 10

line [līn] **58** 25

lines [līnz] **79**

linesman [līnz/ mən] **82** 17

lion [lī/ ən] **68** 3

lip [lĭp] **4** 43

lipstick [lĭp/ stĭk/] **23** 29

liquor (bottle) [lĭk/ ər bŏt/ əl] **16** 22

listen [lĭs/ ən] **77** 6

little finger [lĭt/ əl fĭng/ gər] **4** 28

little league baseball [lĭt/ əl lēg bās/ böl] **92**

Little Leaguer [lĭt/ əl lēg/ ər] **92** 8

little toe [lĭt/ əl tō/] **5** 55

liver [lĭv/ ər] **5** 65

livestock [līv/ stŏk/] **81** 12

living quarters [lĭv/ ĭng kwör/ tərz] **75** 11

living room [lĭv/ ĭng rōōm/] **28**

lizard [lĭz/ ərd] **65** 15

llama [lŏm/ ə] **66** 15

loaf [lōf] **12** 7

loafer [lō/ fər] **21** 42

lobby [lŏb/ ē] **44** 2

lobster [lŏb/ stər] **11** 30, **62** 13

lock [lŏk] **52** 13

locker [lŏk/ ər] **76** 6

locksmith [lŏk/ smĭth/] **85** 4

log [lög] **28** 10

long [löng] **24** 2

long johns [löng/ jŏnz/] **22** 7

long sleeve [löng/ slēv/] **20** 15

loose [lōōs] **24** 4

(loose-leaf) paper [lōōs/ lēf pā/ pər] **76** 13

loudspeaker [lowd/ spē/ kər] **76** 3

Louisiana [lōō ē/ zē ăn/ ə] **72** 18

lounge chair [lownj/ chër/] **27** 24

low [lō] **24** 12

lunar eclipse [lōō/ nər ĭ klĭps/] **74** 6

lunar module [lōō/ nər mŏj/ ōōl] **75** 7

lunch box [lŭnch/ bŏks/] **20** 31

lunch truck [lŭnch/ trŭk/] **49** 8

lung [lŭng] **5** 63

machine gun [mə shēn/ gŭn/] **48** 25

magazine [măg/ ə zēn/] **47** 16

magnet [măg/ nət] **78** 27

magnifying glass [măg/ nə fĭ ĭng glăs/] **78** 15

magnolia [măg nōl/ yə] **61** 29

mail [māl] **46** 2

mail slot [māl/ slŏt/] **46** 13

mail truck [māl/ trŭk/] **46** 5

mailbag [māl/ băg/] **46** 4

mailbox [māl/ bŏks/] **46** 1

Maine [mān] **72** 19

maintenance [mān/ tə nəns] **85**

make (the bed) [māk/ dhə bĕd/] **38** 8

makeup [māk/ ŭp/] **23**

mallet [măl/ ĭt] **36** 11

mammals [măm/ əlz] **66-69**

man [măn] **2** 2

manager [măn/ ĭ jər] **83** 18

mandolin [măn/ də lĭn/] **98** 4

mane [mān] **66** 21a

mango [măng/ gō] **8** 5

manhole [măn/ hōl/] **45** 32

mantel [măn/ təl] **28** 7

mantis [măn/ tĭs] **63** 7

manual transmission [măn/ yōō əl trănz mĭsh/ ən] **50**

map [măp] **70**

maple [mā/ pəl] **61** 38

marigold [măr/ ə gōld/] **60** 6

marine [mə rēn/] **48** 18

Marines [mə rēnz/] **48** 17

Mars [märz] **74** 14

Maryland [mër/ ə lənd] **72** 20

mascara [mă skăr/ ə] **23** 28

mashed potatoes [măsht/ pə tā tōz] **18** 17

mask [măsk] **91** 35

Massachusetts [măs/ ə chōō/ sĭts] **72** 21

mast [măst] **59** 8

mat [măt] **50** 22

matches [măch/ əz] **16** 28

material [mə tïr/ ē əl] **101** 4

math [măth] **79**

mattress [mă/ trəs] **32** 17

measurement [mĕzh/ ər mənt] **79**

meat [mēt] **10**

meatballs [mēt/ bölz/] **18** 11

mechanic [mə kăn/ ĭk] **84** 2

media [mē/ dē ə] **86**

medical care [mĕd/ ə kəl kër/] **39**

medicine [mĕd/ ə sən] **41**

medicine chest [mĕd/ ə sən chĕst/] **34** 14

medicine dropper [mĕd/ ə sən drŏp/ ər] **78** 26

Mediterranean Sea [mĕd/ ĭ tə rā/ nē ən sē/] **70** 24

melon [mĕl/ ən] **9** 35

menu [mĕn/ yōō] **16** 7

Mercury [mür/ kyə rē] **74** 11

merry-go-round [mër/ ē gō rownd/] **87** 5

message pad [mĕs/ ĭj păd/] **83** 25

messenger [mĕs/ ən jər] **86** 19

metal detector [mĕt/ əl də tĕk/ tər] **56** 10

meteor [mē/ tē ər] **74** 5

meter [mē/ tər] **55** 23

mezzanine [mĕz/ ə nēn/] **99** 13

Michigan [mĭsh/ ə gən] **72** 22

microfilm [nī/ krə fĭlm/] **47** 13

microfilm reader [mī/ krə fĭlm rē/ dər] **47** 14

microscope [mī/ krə skōp/] **78** 30

microwave oven [mī/ krə wāv ŭv/ ən] **30** 23

middle finger [mĭd/ əl fĭng/ gər] **4** 26

milk [mĭlk] **14** 5

Minicam™ [mĭn/ ē kăm/] **100** 2

Minnesota [mĭn/ ə sō/ tə] **72** 23

mirror [mïr/ ər] **32** 5

Mississippi [mĭs/ ə sĭp/ ē] **72** 24

Mississippi River [mĭs/ ə sĭp/ ē rĭv/ ər] **71** 58

Missouri [mĭ zŏŏr/ ē] **73** 25

mitt [mĭt] **27** 20

mittens [mĭt/ ənz] **19** 11

mixed vegetables [mĭkst′ vĕj′ tə bəlz] **18** 16

mixing bowl [mĭk′ sĭng bōl′] **30** 24

mobile [mō′ bēl] **33** 2

model [mŏd′ əl] **86** 5

Mojave Desert [mō hŏv′ ē dĕz′ ərt] **71** 48

money [mŭn′ ē] **12**

money order [mŭn′ ē ör′ dər] **46** 18

monitor [mŏn′ ə tər] **100** 32

monkey [mŭng′ ke] **69** 14

monkey wrench [mŭng′ kē rĕnch′] **36** 12

monorail [mŏn′ ə rāl′] **55** 29

Montana [mŏn tăn′ ə] **73** 26

Moon [mōōn] **74** 9

mooring [mŏŏr′ ĭng] **59** 19

moose [mōōs] **67** 35

mop [mŏp] **35** 6

(mop) refill [mŏp′ rē′ fĭl] **35** 11

mortar [mör′ tər] **48** 28

mosquito [mə skē′ tō] **63** 13

motel [mō tĕl′] **90** 3

moth [mŏth] **63** 21

mother [mŭdh′ ər] **3** 4

motor oil [mōt′ər oyl′] **80** 33

motor scooter [mōt′ ər skōō′ tər] **52** 29

motorboat [mōt′ ər bōt′] **59** 13

motorcycle [mōt′ər sī′ kəl] **52** 30, **53** 19

mountain [mown′ tən] **89** 19

mountain climbing [mown′ tən klīm′ ĭng] **89**

mountain ranges [mown′ tən rān′ jəz] **71**

mouse [mows] **66** 9

mousetrap [mows′ trăp′] **35** 32

mouth [mowth] **4** 2

mover [mōō′ vər] **49** 12

movie camera [mōō′ vē kăm′ ə rə] **100** 15

moving van [mōō′ vĭng văn′] **49** 11

mow [mō] **26** 6

mum [mŭm] **60** 4

muscle [mŭs′ əl] **5** 62

mushroom(s) [mŭsh′ rōōm(z)] **7** 30

music [myōō′ zĭk] **99**

musical comedy [myōō′ zə kəl kŏm′ ə dē] **99**

musical instruments [myōō′ zə kəl ĭn′ strə mənts] **98**

musician [myōō zĭsh′ ən] **99** 10

mussel(s) [mŭs′ əl(z)] **11** 34, **62** 3

mustache [mŭs′ tăsh] **4** 40

mustard [mŭs′ tərd] **18** 1

nail [nāl] **37** 41

nail clippers [nāl′ klĭp′ ərz] **23** 31

nail polish [nāl′ pŏl′ ĭsh] **23** 25

nailbrush [nāl′ brŭsh′] **34** 20

napkin [năp′ kĭn] **29** 14

natural gas [năch′ ər əl găs′] **80** 29

Navy [nā′ vē] **48** 13

Nebraska [nə brăs′ kə] **73** 27

neck [nĕk] **4** 4

necklace [nĕk′ lĭs] **23** 6

nectarine [nĕk′ tə rēn′] **8** 17

needle [nē′ dəl] **39** 26, **60** 34a, **101** 18

needlecrafts [nē′ dəl krăfts′] **101**

needlepoint [nē′ dəl poynt′] **101** 26

neighborhood parks [nā′ bər hŏŏd pärks′] **87**

nephew [nĕf′ yōō] **3** 13

Neptune [nĕp′ tōōn] **74** 18

nest [nĕst] **64** 31

net [nĕt] **92** 23

Nevada [nə văd′ ə] **73** 28

new [nōō] **24** 13

New Hampshire [nōō′ hămp′ shər] **72** 29

New Jersey [nōō′ jür′ ze] **73** 30

New Mexico [nōō′ mĕk′ sə kō] **73** 31

new moon [nōō′ mōōn′] **74** 26

New York [nōō′ york′] **73** 32

newscaster [nōōz′ kăs′ tər] **86** 2

newspaper [nōōz′ pā′ pər] **21** 48

newsstand [nōōz′ stănd′] **45** 30

next to [nĕkst′ tōō] **102** 11

nickel [nĭk′ əl] **13** 28

niece [nēs] **3** 14

Niger River [nī′ jər rĭv′ ər] **71** 61

night table [nīt′ tā′ bəl] **32** 27

nightgown [nīt′ gown′] **22** 21

nightstick [nīt′ stĭk′] **43** 9

Nile River [nīl′ rĭv′ ər] **71** 63

nipple [nĭp′ əl] **33** 18

north [nörth] **71** 71

North America [nörth′ə mër′ ə kə] **70** 1

North Atlantic [nörth′ ăt lăn′ tĭk] **70** 11

North Carolina [nörth′ kăr ə lī′ nə] **73** 33

North Dakota [nörth′ də kō′ tə] **73** 34

North Pacific [nörth′ pə sĭf′ ĭk] **70** 9

North Sea [nörth′ sē′] **70** 21

nose [nōz] **4** 36, **57** 8

nostril [nŏs′ trĭl] **4** 37

nozzle [nŏz′ əl] **42** 17

nuclear reactor [nōō′ klē ər rē ăk′ tər] **80** 13

nurse [nürs] **39** 19

nut [nŭt] **37** 39

nuts [nŭts] **9**

oak [ōk] **61** 33

oar [ör] **59** 22

oarlock [ör′ lŏk′] **59** 21

oats [ōts] **60** 23

Ob River [ŏb′ rĭv′ ər] **71** 64

oboe [ō′ bō] **98** 15

obtuse angle [ŏb tōōs′ ăng′ gəl] **79** 5

occupations [ŏk′ yə pā′ shənz] **84-86**

ocean liner [ō′ shən lī′ nər] **58** 27

oceans [ō′ shənz] **70**

octopus [ŏk′ tə pəs] **62** 6

office [ö′ fĭs] **83**

office building [ö′ fĭs bĭl′ dĭng] **44** 1

officer [ö′ fĭ sər] **86** 13

Ohio [ō hī′ ō] **73** 35

oil [oyl] **38** 12

oil well [oyl′ wĕl′] **80** 1

ointment [oynt′ mənt] **41** 9

Oklahoma [ō′ klə hō′ mə] **73** 36

old [ōld] **24** 14

on [ŏn] **102** 5

on top of [ŏn tŏp′ əv] **102** 10

onion(s) [ŭn′ yən(z)] **7** 31

open [ō′ pən] **24** 15, **31** 3

optician [ŏp tĭsh′ ən] **84** 9

oral hygienist [ör′ əl hī jē′ nĭst] **39** 14

orange [ör′ ĭnj] **8** 8

orangutan [ə răng′ ə tăn′] **69** 18

orbit [ör′ bĭt] **74** 21

orchard [ör′ chərd] **81** 1

orchestra [ör′ kə strə] **99** 6

orchestra seating [ör′ kə strə sēt′ ĭng] **99** 12

orchid [ör′ kĭd] **60** 12

order [ör′ dər] **17** 5

Oregon [ör′ ə gən] **73** 37

organ [ör′ gən] **98** 29

ostrich [ŏs′ trĭch] **64** 12

otter [ŏt′ ər] **68** 10

out of [owt′ əv] **103** 7

outboard motor [owt′ börd mō′ tər] **59** 12

outer space [owt′ ər spās′] **74**

outlet [owt′ lət] **36** 6

oval [ō′ vəl] **79** 18

oven [ŭv′ ən] **30** 32

over [ō′ vər] **103** 8

overalls [ō′ vər ölz′] **21** 30

overcoat [ō′ vər kōt′] **19** 20

overhead projector
  [ō′ vər hĕd prə jĕk′ tər] **76** 27

overpass [ō′ vər păs′] **53** 3

owl [owl] **64** 6

oyster(s) [oy′ stər(z)] **11** 33, **62** 2

pacifier [păs′ ə fī′ ər] **33** 22

pack [păk] **13** 16

package [păk′ ĭj] **12** 4, **46** 19

pad [păd] **83** 26

paddle [păd′ əl] **59** 3, **94** 18

pail [pāl] **90** 16

paint (v) [pānt] **26** 1

paint (n) [pānt] **37** 31

paintbrush [pānt′ brŭsh′] **37** 30

Painted Desert [pān′ təd dez′ ərt] **71** 49

painter [pān′ tər] **85** 7

painting [pān′ tĭng] **28** 5

(pair of) scissors [pĕr′ əv sĭz′ ərz]
  101 17

pajamas [pə jŏm′ əz] **22** 19

palm [pŏm] **4** 29, **61** 26

pan [păn] **37** 28

pancakes [păn′ kāks′] **18** 5

pancreas [pang′ krē əs] **5** 71

panda [păn də] **69** 20

panel truck [păn′ əl trŭk′] **49** 9

pansy [păn′ zē] **60** 2

panties [păn′ tēz] **22** 11

pants [pănts] **21** 27

pantyhose [păn′ tē hōz′] **22** 5

papaya [pə pī′ yə] **8** 6

paper [pā′ pər] **76** 13

paper clips [pā′ pər klĭps′] **83** 28

paper towels [pā′ pər tow′əlz] **35** 23

parachute [păr′ ə shōot′] **48** 6

parakeet [păr′ ə kēt] **64** 15

parallel lines [păr′ ə lĕl līnz′] **79** 4

paramedic [păr′ ə mĕd′ ĭk] **42** 7

Parana River [păr′ ə nŏ′ rĭv′ ər] **71** 60

parents [păr′ ənts] **2** 6

park [pärk] **87**

park ranger [pärk′ rān′ jər] **88** 5

parka [pär′ kə] **19** 8

parking lights [pär′ kĭng līts′] **51** 49

parking garage [pär′ kĭng gə rŏj′]
  45 19

parking meter [pär′ kĭng mē′ tər]
  45 20

parrot [păr′ ət] **64** 16

part [pärt] **4** 31

pass [păs] **96** 5

passenger [păs′ ĭn jər] **55** 25

passenger car [păs′ ĭn jər kär′] **53** 15

pasture [păs′ chər] **81** 6

patient [pā′shənt] **39** 20

patio [păt′ ē ō′] **27** 17

pattern [păt′ ərn] **101** 7

pattern piece [păt′ ərn pēs′] **101** 6

paw [pö] **69** 29a

pay [pā] **17** 7

pea(s) [pē(z)] **6** 17

peach [pēch] **9** 37

peacock [pē′ kŏk′] **64** 18

peak [pēk] **89** 20

peanut(s) [pē′ nŭt(s)′] **9** 28

pear [pĕr] **8** 18

pedal [pĕd′ əl] **39** 18, **52** 19

pedestrian [pə dĕs′ trē ən] **44** 12

peel (n) [pēl] **9** 20a

peel (v) [pēl] **31** 5

pegboard [pĕg′ börd′] **36** 15

pelican [pĕl′ ə kən] **64** 24

pencil [pĕn′ səl] **76** 24

pencil eraser [pĕn′ səl ə rā′ sər] **76** 21

pencil sharpener
  [pĕn′ səl shär′ pə nər] **76** 20, **83** 30

Pennsylvania [pĕn səl vān′ yə] **73** 38

penny [pĕn′ ē] **13** 27

penguin [pĕn′ gwĭn] **64** 27

people [pē′ pəl] **2**

pepper shaker [pĕp′ ər shā′ kər] **29** 9

pepper(s) [pĕp′ ər(z)] **7** 22

percussion [pər kŭsh′ ən] **98**

perfume [pür′ fyōom] **23** 27

periodicals section
  [pïr′ ē ŏd′ ə kəlz sĕk′ shən] **47** 15

periscope [pĕr′ə skōp′] **48** 8

perpendicular lines
  [pür′ pən dĭk′ yə lər līnz′] **79** 2

Persian Gulf [pür′ zhən gŭlf ′] **70** 28

personal computer (PC)
  [pür′ sə nəl kŭm pyōo′ tər]/
  [pē′ sē′] **100** 31

personnel [pür′ sə nĕl′] **48**

petal [pĕt′ əl] **60** 18b

petri dish [pēt′ rē dĭsh′] **78** 3

petunia [pə tōon′ yə] **60** 7

pharmacist [fär′ mə sĭst] **84** 1

phases of the moon
  [fā′ zəz əv dhə mōon′] **74**

pheasant [fĕz′ ənt] **64** 19

Phillips screwdriver
  [fĭl′ ĭps skrōo′ drī vər] **37** 25

phone [fōn] **32** 26

photocopier [fō′ tə kŏp′ ē ər] **83** 24

photocopy machine
  [fō tə kŏp ē mə shēn′] **47** 18

photographer [fə tŏg′ rə fər] **86** 4

photography [fə tŏg′ rə fē] **100**

piano [pē ăn′ ō] **98** 1

piccolo [pĭk′ ə lō′] **98** 12

pick (v) [pĭk] **26** 7

pick (n) [pĭk] **98** 11a

pickup truck [pĭk′ ŭp trŭk′] **49** 4

pickax [pĭk′ ăks′] **82** 13

pickle [pĭk′ əl] **18** 8

picnic area [pĭk′nĭk ër′ ē ə] **88**

picnic basket [pĭk′ nĭk băs′ kət] **88** 13

picnic table [pĭk′ nĭk tā′ bəl] **88** 15

piece [pēs] **12** 22

pier [pïr] **58** 3

pierced earring [pïrst′ ïr′ ĭng] **23** 16

pigeon [pĭj′ ən] **64** 1

pill [pĭl] **41** 7

pillow [pĭl′ ō] **32** 16

pillowcase [pĭl′ ō kās′] **32** 15

pilot [pī′ lət] **56** 15
pin [pĭn] **23** 8, **94** 5, **101** 20
pincushion [pĭn′ koŏsh′ ən] **101** 3
pine [pīn] **60** 34
pineapple [pīn′ ăp′ əl] **8** 4
ping-pong [pĭng′ pŏng′] **94**
ping-pong ball [pĭng′ pŏng böl′] **94** 19
pinking shears [pĭng′ kĭng shïrz′]
   101 5
pipe [pīp] **16** 26, **35** 18
pipette [pī pĕt′] **78** 14
pit [pĭt] **8** 37a
pitcher [pĭch′ ər] **29** 4, **93** 12
pitcher's mound [pĭch′ ərz mownd′]
   93 11
pitchfork [pĭch′ förk′] **81** 14
pizza [pēt′ sə] **18** 30
plaid [plăd] **24** 22
plane [plān] **57** 18
planets [plăn′ əts] **74**
plant (v) [plănt] **26** 4
plants (n) [plănts] **60**
plate [plāt] **29** 13
plateau [plă tō′] **88** 1
platform [plăt′ förm′] **54** 11
playground [plā′ grownd′] **87** 15
playpen [plā′ pĕn′] **33** 30
pleasure boating [plĕzh′ ər bō′ tĭng] **59**
pliers [plī′ ərz] **36** 19
plug [plŭg] **37** 43d
plum [plŭm] **9** 34
plumber [plŭm′ ər] **85** 1
plunger [plŭn′ jər] **35** 14
Pluto [ploo′ tō] **74** 19
pocket [pŏk′ ət] **21** 41
pod [pŏd] **6** 17a
podium [pō′ dē əm] **99** 7
poinsettia [poyn sĕt′ē ə] **60** 15
poison ivy [poy′ zən ī′ vē] **61** 45
poison oak [poy′ zən ōk′] **61** 43
poison sumac [poy′ zən soo′ măk]
   61 44
poisonous plants [poy′ zə nəs plănts′]
   61
polar bear [pōl′ ər bër′] **69** 22
pole [pōl] **94** 34, **95** 14
police officer [pə lēs′ öf′ ə sər] **43** 6
police station [pə lēs′ stā′ shən] **43**

polish [pŏl′ ĭsh] **38** 3
polka dot [pō′ kə dŏt′] **24** 19
pond [pŏnd] **87** 8
pony [pō′ nē] **67** 20
poplar [pŏp′ lər] **61** 30
porch [pörch] **27** 6
porcupine [pör′ kyə pīn′] **66** 11
pork [pörk] **10** 6
pork chops [pörk′ chŏps′] **18** 15
port [pört] **58**
porter [pör′ tər] **56** 5
porthole [pört′ hōl′] **58** 21
post [pōst] **23** 18
post office [pōst′ öf′ ĭs] **44** 9, **46**
postal worker [pōs′ təl wür′ kər] **46** 14
postcard [pōst′ kärd′] **46** 17
postmark [pōst′ märk′] **46** 9
pot [pŏt] **30** 13
pot holder [pŏt′ hōl′ dər] **30** 34
potato chips [pə tā′ tō chĭps′] **18** 4
potato(es) [pə tā′ tō(z)] **7** 23
potty [pŏt′ ē] **33** 33
pouch [powch] **66** 3c
pouched mammals [powcht′ măm′ əlz]
   66
poultry [pōl′ trē] **10**
pour [pör] **31** 4
power lines [pow′ ər līnz′] **80** 24
power sander [pow′ ər săn′ dər] **37** 26
power saw [pow′ ər sö′] **27** 25
power station [pow′ ər stā′ shən] **80** 20
prepositions [prep′ ə zĭ′ shənz]
   102, **103**
primates [prī′ māts] **69**
print [prĭnt] **24** 21
printer [prĭn′ tər] **83** 4
printout [prĭnt′ owt′] **83** 8
prints [prĭnts] **100** 11
prism [prĭz′ əm] **78** 1
private jet [prī′ vət jĕt′] **57** 3
produce [prŏd′ oōs] **14** 9
programs [prō′ grămz] **99** 17
projector [prə jĕk′ tər] **100** 16
propane gas [prō′ pān găs′] **80** 30
propeller plane [prə pĕl′ ər plān′] **57** 7
prosecuting attorney
   [prŏ′ sə kyoō tĭng ə tür′ nē] **43** 17
prune [proōn] **9** 22

public library [pŭb′ lĭk lī′ brër ē] **47**
public transportation
   [pŭb′ lĭk trăns pər tā′ shən] **54**
public telephone [pŭb′ lĭk tĕl′ ə fōn]
   44 7
puck [pŭk] **92** 17
pump [pŭmp] **13** 14, **52** 21
pumpkin [pŭmp′ kĭn] **7** 26
punishment [pŭn′ ĭsh mənt] **43**
pupil [pyoō′ pəl] **5** 48
puppy [pŭp′ ē] **69** 27
purse [pürs] **20** 23
push [poŏsh] **26** 12
putter [pŭt′ ər] **94** 9
puzzle [pŭz′ əl] **33** 31
pyramid [pïr′ ə mĭd′] **79** 25
quantities [kwŏn′ tə tēz] **12**
quarter [kwör′ tər] **11** 18, **13** 30,
   79 31
quarterback [kwör′ tər băk′] **93** 32
quill [kwĭl] **66** 11a
quilting [kwĭl′ tĭng] **101** 32
rabbit [răb′ ĭt] **66** 13
raccoon [ră koōn′] **68** 7
race track [rās′ trăk′] **95**
(racing) handlebars
   [rā′ sĭng hăn′ dəl bärz] **52** 2
rack [răk] **47** 17, **78** 8
racket [răk′ ĭt] **94** 2
racquet [răk′ ĭt] **94** 29
racquetball [răk′ ĭt böl′] **94** 30
radiator [rā′ dē āt′ ər] **51** 56
radio [rā′ dē ō′] **50** 18
radish(es) [răd′ ĭsh (əz)] **7** 29
radius [rā′ dē əs] **79** 14
raft [răft] **89** 16
rafters [răf′ tərz] **82** 1
rafting [răf′ tĭng] **89**
rags [răgz] **35** 4
rain boots [rān′ boōts′] **19** 25
raincoat [rān′ kōt′] **21** 38
rainy [rān′ ē] **25** 1
raise (one's hand) [rāz′ wŭnz hănd′]
   77 1
raisin(s) [rā′ zən(z)] **9** 24
rake (v) [rāk] **26** 10
rake (n) [rāk] **27** 30
ranch [rănch] **81**

ranch house [rănch′ hows′] **27**

ranching [rănch′ ĭng] **81**

rapids [răp′ ĭdz] **89** 17

rash [răsh] **40** 1

raspberries [răz′ bër′ ēz] **8** 16

rat [răt] **66** 7

rattle [răt′ əl] **33** 21

rattlesnake [răt′ əl snāk′] **65** 10

razor [rā′ zər] **23** 20

razor blades [rā′ zər blādz′] **23** 23

read [rēd] **77** 4

real estate agent [rēl′ ə stāt ā′ jənt] **85** 5

rear bumper [rïr′ bŭm′ pər] **50** 42

rearview mirror [rïr′ vyōō mïr′ ər] **50** 7

receipt [rə sēt′] **15** 20, **55** 24

receiver [rə sē′ vər] **100** 21

receptionist [rə sĕp′ shə nəst] **86** 17

recliner [rə klī′ nər] **28** 16

records [rĕk′ ərdz] **100** 23

rectangle [rĕk′ tăng′ gəl] **79** 19

Red Sea [rĕd′ sē′] **70** 29

redwood [rĕd′ wŏŏd′] **61** 25

(reel of) film [rel′ əv fĭlm′] **100** 17

referee [rĕf′ ə rē′] **93** 22, **94** 16

reference section [rĕf′ ə rəns sĕk′ shən] **47** 21

(reference) librarian [rĕf′ ə rəns lī brër′ e ən] **47** 23

refill [rē′ fĭl′] **35** 11

refinery [rə fī′ nə rē] **80** 12

reflector [rə flĕk′ tər] **52** 25

refreshment stand [rə frĕsh′ mənt stănd′] **90** 2

refrigerator [rə frĭj′ ə rā′ tər] **30** 19

reins [rānz] **94** 22

relationships [rə lā′ shən ships′] **2**

remedies [rĕm′ ə dēz] **41**

remote control [rə mōt′ kən trōl′] **28** 17

repair [rə për′] **38** 10

repairperson [rə për′ pür′ sən] **84** 5

reporter [rə pör′ tər] **86** 11

reptiles [rĕp′ tĭlz] **65**

rescue [rĕs′ kyōō] **42**

restaurant [rĕs′ tə rənt] **16**

retriever [rə trē′ vər] **69** 26

return address [rə türn′ ă drĕs′] **46** 8

rhinoceros [rī nŏs′ ə rəs] **66** 16

Rhode Island [rōd′ ī′ lənd] **73** 39

rice [rīs] **60** 21

ride [rīd] **97** 13

rider [rī′ dər] **54** 6

rifle [rī′ fəl] **48** 21

right angle [rīt′ ăng′ gəl] **79** 23

right fielder [rīt′ fēl′ dər] **93** 3

right guard [rīt′ gärd′] **93** 28

right lane [rīt′ lān′] **53** 7

right tackle [rīt′ tăk′ əl] **93** 29

right triangle [rīt′ trī′ ăng gəl] **79** 22

rind [rīnd] **8** 8b

ring(s) [rĭng(z)] **23** 2, **74** 16a, **94** 17

ring binder [rĭng′ bīn′ dər] **76** 14

ring finger [rĭng′ fĭng′ gər] **4** 27

ring stand [rĭng′ stănd′] **78** 19

rink [rĭngk] **94** 25

Rio Grande River [rē′ ō grănd′ rĭv′ ər] **71** 57

rivers [riv′ ərz] **71**

road sign [rōd′ sīn′] **53** 23

road work [rōd′ würk′] **82**

roadrunner [rōd′ rŭn′ ər] **64** 32

roast [rōst] **10** 3, **10** 8

roasting pan [rōs′ tĭng păn′] **30** 17

robes [rōbz] **43** 11

robin [rŏb′ in] **64** 9

rock group [rŏk′ grōōp′] **99**

rocket [rŏk′ ət] **75** 13

rocks [rŏks] **88** 11

rocking chair [rŏk′ ĭng chër′] **33** 16

Rocky Mountains [rŏk′ ē mown′ tənz] **71** 40

rodents [rō′ dənts] **66**

roll [rōl] **12** 11, **18** 19

(roll of) film [rōl′ əv fĭlm′] **100** 10

roller [rōl′ ər] **37** 29

rolling pin [rōl′ ĭng pĭn′] **30** 25

rolodex [rōl′ ə dĕks′] **83** 14

rooster [rōō′ stər] **64** 21

roof [rōōf] **27** 4

root [rōōt] **60** 35d

rope [rōp] **89** 23

rose [rōz] **60** 18

rotor [rō′ tər] **57** 2a

rough [rŭf] **95** 6

router [row′ tər] **37** 37

row [rō] **47** 11, **81** 18

rowboat [rō′ bōt′] **59** 23

Rub′ al Khali Desert [rōōb′ ăl kŏl′ ē dĕz′ ərt] **71** 52

rubber tubing [rŭb′ ər tōōb′ ĭng] **78** 18

rudder [rŭd′ ər] **59** 5

rug [rŭg] **32** 28

ruler [rōō′ lər] **76** 23

run [rŭn] **96** 6

rung [rŭng] **82** 9

runner [rŭn′ ər] **91** 23, **94** 31

runway [rŭn′ wā′] **57** 19

saddle [săd′ əl] **94** 20

safety glasses [sāf′ tē glăs′ əz] **78** 12

safety goggles [sāf′ tē gŏg′ əlz] **94** 28

safety pin [sāf′ tē pĭn′] **33** 11

Sahara Desert [sə hër′ ə dĕz′ ərt] **71** 51

sail [sāl] **59** 9

sailboard [sāl′ börd′] **59** 15

sailboat [sāl′ bōt′] **59** 4

sailor [sāl′ ər] **48** 14

salad bowl [săl′ əd bōl′] **29** 25

salad dressing [săl′ əd drĕs′ ĭng] **18** 12

salamander [săl′ ə măn′ dər] **65** 14

salesperson [sālz′ pür′ sən] **86** 12

salt shaker [sölt′ shā′ kər] **29** 10

sand (v) [sănd] **26** 14

sand (n) [sănd] **90** 31

sand dunes [sănd′ dōōnz′] **90** 12

sand trap [sănd′ trăp′] **95** 11

sandal [săn′ dəl] **20** 19

sandbox [sănd′ bŏks′] **87** 13

sandcastle [sănd′ kăs′ əl] **91** 32

sandpaper [sănd′ pā′ pər] **37** 27

sandwich [sănd′ wĭch] **16** 16

sanitation worker [săn ə tā′ shən wür′ kər] **49** 7

Saturn [săt′ ərn] **74** 16

saucepan [sös′ păn′] **30** 8

saucer [sö′ sər] **29** 21

sausage [sö′ sĭj] **10** 7

saw [sö] **36** 8

saxophone [săk′ sə fōn′] **98** 24

scaffolding [skăf′ əl dĭng] **82** 7

scale [skāl] **14** 7, **34** 32, **78** 4

scallop(s) [skăl′ əp(s)] **11** 35, **62** 10

scarecrow [skër/ krō/] **81** 19
scarf [skärf] **19** 19
scenery [sē/ nə rē] **99** 2
school [skool] **76, 77**
science lab [sī/ əns lăb/] **78**
scissors [sĭz/ərz] **101** 17
scoreboard [skör/ börd/] **93** 19
scorpion [skör/ pē ən] **63** 8
scouring pad [skowr/ ĭng păd/] **30** 11
scrape [skrāp] **26** 15
scraper [skrāp/ ər] **36** 14
screen [skrēn] **27** 19, **100** 14
screw [skroo] **37** 42
screwdriver [skroo/ drī/ vər] **37** 24
scrub [skrŭb] **38** 2
scuba tank [skoo/ bə tăngk/] **91** 37
sea gull [sē/ gŭl/] **64** 4
sea horse [sē/ hörs/] **65** 1
Sea of Japan [sē/ əv jə păn/] **70** 36
Sea of Okhotsk [sē/ əv ō kŏtsk/]
    70 35
seafood [sē/ food/] **10**
seal [sēl] **68** 12
seam [sēm] **101** 10
seas [sēz] **70**
seat [sēt] **52** 16, **54** 2
seat belt [sēt/ bĕlt] **50** 23
second baseman [sĕk/ ənd bās/ mən]
    93 7
secretary [sĕk/ rə tĕr/ ē] **83** 11
section [sĕk/ shən] **8** 8a, **79** 15
security [sə kyoor/ ə tē] **56**
security guard [sə kyoor/ ə tē gärd/]
    56 9, **86** 14
sedan [sə dăn/] **51**
seed [sēd] **8** 8c
seesaw [sē/ sö/] **87** 18
serve [sürv] **17** 3, **96** 2
service area [sür/ vəs ër/ ē ə] **53** 11
sevice court [sür/ vəs kört/] **95** 1
service line [sür/ vəs līn/] **95** 3
set (the table) [sĕt/ dhə tā/ bəl] **17** 8
sewing [sō/ ĭng] **101**
sewing machine [sō/ ĭng mə shēn/]
    101 1
shade [shād] **33** 1
shaft [shăft] **80** 10
shampoo [shăm poo/] **34** 8

shank [shănk] **37** 43b
shark [shärk] **65** 5
shaving cream [shā/ vĭng krēm/] **23** 22
sheep [shēp] **67** 25, **81** 10
sheet [shēt] **32** 19
sheet music [shēt/ myoo/ zĭk] **98** 2
shelf [shĕlf] **14** 6, **47** 26
shell [shĕl] **48** 27, **62** 1a, **65** 18a,
    90 40
shellfish [shĕl/ fĭsh/] **11**
shepherd [shĕp/ ərd] **69** 28
shingle [shĭng/ gəl] **82** 2
ship [shĭp] **58** 9
shirt [shürt] **21** 46
shock absorbers [shŏk/ əb zör/ bərz]
    52 31
shoe [shoo] **21** 49
shoelace [shoo/ lās/] **20** 7
shoot [shoot] **97** 16
shop worker [shŏp/ wür/ kər] **85** 12
shopping bag [shŏp/ ĭng băg/] **20** 18
shopping basket [shŏp/ ĭng băs/ kət]
    14 8
shopping cart [shŏp/ ĭng kärt/] **15** 19
short [shört] **24** 1
short sleeve [shört/ slēv/] **20** 21
shorts [shörts] **20** 14
shortstop [shört/ stŏp/] **93** 5
shoulder [shōl/ dər] **4** 5, **53** 22
(shoulder) bag [shōl/ dər băg/] **21** 35
shovel (n) [shŭv/ əl] **27** 31, **82** 15,
    90 17
shovel (v) [shŭv/ əl] **26** 13
shower cap [show/ ər kăp/] **34** 3
shower curtain [show/ ər kür/ tən] **34** 5
shower head [show/ ər hĕd/] **34** 4
shrimp [shrĭmp] **11** 31, **62** 8
shutter [shŭt/ ər] **27** 8
shuttle car [shŭt/ əl kär/] **80** 8
side [sīd] **79** 10
side mirror [sīd/ mïr/ ər] **50** 2
sideburn [sīd/ bürn/] **4** 33
sidewalk [sīd/ wök/] **45** 25
Sierra Madre [sē ër/ ə mŏ/ drē] **71** 42
silo [sī/ lō] **81** 4
silverware [sĭl/ vər wër/] **29** 22
simple animals [sĭm/ pəl ăn/ ə məlz] **62**
singer [sĭng/ ər] **99** 24

sink [sĭngk] **34** 19
sister [sĭs/ tər] **3** 10
sister-in-law [sĭs/ tər ən lö/] **3** 8
six-pack [sĭks/ păk/] **13** 13
skate (n) [skāt] **94** 26
skate (v) [skāt] **97** 9
skein [skān] **101** 24
ski [skē] **95** 17
ski boot [skē/ boot/] **95** 15
ski cap [skē/ kăp/] **19** 16
ski lift [skē/ lĭft/] **95** 18
ski slope [skē/ slōp/] **95**
skier [skē/ ər] **94** 35
skis [skēz] **94** 33
skin [skĭn] **9** 37b
skirt [skürt] **21** 36
skunk [skŭngk] **68** 8
slacks [slăks] **20** 4
sleeping bag [slē/ pĭng băg/] **89** 26
sleepwear [slēp/ wër/] **22**
slice (n) [slīs] **13** 21
slice (v) [slīs] **31** 10
slide [slīd] **78** 31, **87** 12
slide projector [slīd/ prə jĕk/ tər]
    100 13
slides [slīdz] **100** 12
sling [slĭng] **39** 3
slippers [slĭp/ərz] **22** 18
slug [slŭg] **62** 4
small [smöl] **24** 7
smoke [smōk] **42** 15
smoke detector [smōk/ də tĕk/ tər]
    33 15
smokestack [smōk/ stăk/] **58** 18,
    80 22
snacks [snăks] **14** 18
snail [snāl] **62** 1
snake [snāk] **65** 9
snap [snăp] **101** 13
sneakers [snē/ kərz] **20** 11
snorkel [snör/ kəl] **91** 34
snow plow [snō/ plow/] **49** 5
snowy [snō/ e] **25** 3
soap [sōp] **34** 15
soap dish [sōp/ dĭsh/] **34** 6
soccer [sŏk/ ər] **92**
soccer ball [sŏk/ ər böl/] **92** 26
socks [sŏks] **22** 17

sofa [sō′ fə] **28** 25
soft drink [söft′ drĭngk′] **16** 11
softball [söft′ böl′] **92, 92** 10
solar collector [sō′ lər kə lĕk′ tər] **80** 17
solar eclipse [sō′ lər ĭ klĭps′] **74** 10
solar system [sō′ lər sĭs′ təm] **74**
soldier [sōl′ jər] **48** 16
sole [sōl] **20** 6
solid [sŏl′ əd] **24** 20
solid figures [sŏl′ əd fĭg′ yərz] **79**
son [sŭn] **3** 16
Sony Walkman [sō′ nē wök′ mən] **100** 30
sore throat [sör′ thrōt′] **40** 12
south [sowth] **71** 72
South America [sowth′ ə mĕr′ ə kə] **70** 2
South Atlantic [sowth′ ăt lăn′ tək] **70** 12
South Carolina [sowth′ kăr ə lī′ nə] **73** 40
South China Sea [sowth′ chi′ nə sē′] **70** 39
South Dakota [sowth′ də kō′ tə] **73** 41
South Pacific [sowth pə sĭf′ ək] **70** 10
space probe [spās′ prōb] **75** 4
space program [spās′ prō′ grăm] **75**
space shuttle [spās′ shŭt′ əl] **75** 14
space station [spās′ stā′ shən] **75** 1
space suit [spās′ sōōt′] **75** 6
spacecraft [spās′ krăft′] **75**
spaghetti [spə gĕt′ ē] **18** 10
spaniel [spăn′ yəl] **69** 24
spare ribs [spĕr′ rĭbz′] **10** 10
spare tire [spĕr′ tīr′] **51** 39
sparrow [spăr′ ō] **64** 10
spatula [spăch′ə lə] **27** 21
speaker [spē′ kər] **28** 21, **100** 24
speed limit sign [spēd′ lĭm ət sīn′] **53** 8
speedometer [spə dŏm′ə tər] **50** 10
spider [spī′ dər] **63** 16
spinach [spĭn′ əch] **6** 8
spinal cord [spī′ nəl körd′] **5** 58
spiral notebook [spī′ rəl nōt′ bŏok] **76** 15
split [splĭt] **11** 17

split end [splĭt′ ĕnd′] **93** 24
spoke [spōk] **52** 26
sponge [spŭnj] **34** 7
(sponge) mop [spŭnj′ mŏp′] **35** 6
(spool of) thread [spōōl′ əv thrĕd′] **101** 2
spoon [spōōn] **29** 8
sports car [spörts′ kär′] **53** 17
sports [spörts] **92-97**
spotlight [spŏt′ līt′] **99** 4
sprain [sprān] **40** 13
spray can [sprā′ kăn′] **13** 24
spray starch [sprā′ stärch′] **35** 21
spread [sprĕd] **17** 11
Spring [sprĭng] **26**
sprinkler [sprĭng′ klər] **27** 13, **87** 14
sprocket [sprŏk′ ət] **52** 20
square [skwĕr] **79** 9
squid [skwĭd] **62** 5
squirrel [skwür′ əl] **66** 10
stage [stāj] **99** 5
staircase [stĕr′ kās] **28** 12
stake [stāk] **89** 30
stamp [stămp] **46** 10
stands [stăndz] **93** 10
staple remover [stāp′ əl rə moo′ vər] **83** 29
stapler [stāp′ lər] **83** 27
star [stär] **74** 4
starfish [stär′ fĭsh′] **62** 7
starting gate [stär′ tĭng gāt′] **95** 20
station [stā′ shən] **55** 18
station wagon [stā′ shən wăg′ ən] **50**
steak [stāk] **10** 5, **11** 29, **18** 21
steam [stēm] **31** 12
steamer [stēm′ ər] **30** 3
steering wheel [stür′ ĭng wēl′] **50** 8
stem [stĕm] **8** 2a, **60** 1a
step [stĕp] **28** 13
stepladder [stĕp′ lăd′ ər] **35** 1
stereo cassette player [stĕr′ ē ō kə sĕt plā′ ər] **100** 25
stereo system [stĕr′ ē ō sīs′ təm] **28** 20
stern [stürn] **58** 11
stethoscope [stĕth′ ə skōp′] **39** 9
stewing meat [stoo′ ĭng mēt] **10** 4
stick [stĭk] **12** 5
stick shift [stĭk′ shĭft′] **50** 24

sting [stĭng] **63** 8a
stingray [stĭng′ rā′] **65** 6
stir [stür] **31** 1
stitch [stĭch] **101** 19
stitches [stĭch′ əz] **39** 21
stockings [stŏk′ ĭngz] **22** 6
stomach [stŭm′ ək] **5** 66
stomachache [stŭm′ ək āk′] **40** 7
stool [stōōl] **78** 34
stopper [stŏp′ ər] **34** 10, **78** 10
stork [störk] **64** 30
stove [stōv] **30** 30
straight line [strāt′ līn′] **79** 1
(strand of) beads [strănd′ əv bēdz′] **23** 7
strap [străp] **54** 8
straw [strö] **16** 10
strawberry [strö′ bĕr′ ē] **8** 15
strawberry shortcake [strö′ bĕr ē shört′ kāk] **18** 26
stream [strēm] **88** 6
street [strēt] **45** 31
street cleaner [strēt′ klē′ nər] **49** 1
street sign [strēt′ sīn′] **44** 8
streetcar [strēt′ kär′] **55** 30
streetlight [strēt′ līt′] **45** 29
stretch [strĕch] **95** 19
stretch bandage [strĕch′ băn′ dĭj] **40** 13a
stretcher [strĕch′ ər] **39** 12
stretchie [strĕch′ ē] **33** 19
string [strĭng] **46** 20, **98** 10a
string bean(s) [strĭng′ bēn(z)′] **6** 15
strings [strĭngz] **98**
striped [strīpt] **24** 17
stroller [strō′ lər] **33** 14
student [stōō′ dənt] **76** 19
stuffed animal [stŭft′ ăn ə məl] **33** 27
subject [sŭb′ jəkt] **47** 10
submarine [sŭb′ mə rēn′] **48** 7
subway [sŭb′ wā′] **54**
subway station [sŭb′ wā stā′ shən] **44** 16
sugar (packet) [shōōg′ ər păk′ ət] **16** 13
sugar bowl [shōōg′ ər bōl′] **29** 23
sugarcane [shōōg′ ər kān′] **60** 20
suitcase [sōōt′ kās′] **56** 7
Summer [sŭm′ ər] **26**

sun [sŭn] **74** 7, **80** 3
sunbather [sŭn/ bā/ dhər] **90** 19
sundae [sŭn/ dē] **18** 23
sunflower [sŭn/ flŏw/ ər] **60** 19
sunglasses [sŭn/ glăs/ əz] **90** 14
sunny [sŭn/ ē] **25** 4
(sunnyside-up) egg
   [sŭn/ ē sīd ŭp/ ĕg/] **18** 32
sunroof [sŭn/ rōof/] **51** 44
suntan lotion [sŭn/ tăn lō/.shən] **91** 39
supermarket [sōo/ pər mär/ kət] **14**
surf [sürf] **97** 12
surfboard [sürf/ börd/] **91** 25
surgery [sŭr/ jə rē] **41** 2
suspect [sŭs/ pĕkt] **43** 3
swan [swŏn] **64** 28
sweatband [swĕt/ bănd/] **20** 12
sweater [swĕt/ ər] **19** 7, **19** 13, **19** 23
sweatpants [swĕt/ pănts/] **20** 10
sweatshirt [swĕt/ shürt/] **20** 8
sweep [swēp] **38** 7
swimmer [swĭm/ ər] **91** 28
swing [swĭng] **33** 24
swings [swĭngz] **87** 16
switch [swĭch] **37** 43c
switchboard [swĭch/ börd/] **83** 3
switchboard operator
   [swĭch/ börd ŏp/ ə rā tər] **83** 1
swordfish [sörd/ fĭsh/] **65** 3
synthesizer [sĭn/ thə sī/ zər] **99** 21
syringe [sə rĭnj/] **39** 27
syrup [sĭr/ əp] **18** 6
T-shirt [tē/ shürt/] **21** 29
table [tā/ bəl] **29** 7
tablecloth [tā/ bəl klöth/] **29** 16
tablet [tāb/ lət] **41** 6
taco [tŏ/ kō] **18** 24
tadpole [tăd/ pōl/] **65** 16
tail [tāl] **57** 10, **65** 3a, **66** 3a
taillight [tāl/ līt/] **50** 31
tailor [tā/ lər] **84** 6
take [tāk] **17** 10
takeoff [tāk/ ŏf/] **57**
Takla Makan Desert
   [tŏk/ lə mə kŏn/ dĕz/ ərt] **71** 53
tambourine [tăm/ bə rēn/] **98** 17
tank [tăngk] **48** 10
tank top [tăngk/ tŏp/] **20** 13

tanker [tăngk/ ər] **58** 15
tap [tăp] **16** 20
tape [tāp] **46** 22
tape measure [tāp/ mĕzh/ ər] **36** 21, **101** 15
taxi [tăk/ sē] **55**
taxi stand [tăk/ sē stănd/] **55** 28
taxicab [tăk/ sē kăb/] **55** 27
tea [tē] **16** 15
teacher [tē/ chər] **76** 4
teakettle [tē/ kĕt/ əl] **30** 28
team sports [tēm/ spörts/] **92**
teapot [tē/ pŏt/] **29** 19
tear [tër] **77** 9
teddy bear [tĕd/ ē bër/] **33** 3
tee [tē] **95** 13
telephone [tĕl/ ə fōn/] **83** 15
telescope [tĕl/ ə skōp/] **74** 22
television [tĕl/ ə vĭzh/ ən] **28** 18, **100** 5
teller [tĕl/ ər] **86** 15
temperature [tĕm/ pər ə chər] **25** 6
Tennessee [tĕn/ ə sē/] **73** 42
tennis [tĕn/ əs] **94**
tennis ball [tĕn/ əs böl/] **94** 1
tennis court [tĕn/ əs kört/] **95**
tent [tĕnt] **89** 24
tentacle [tĕn/ tə kəl] **62** 12a
terminal [türm/ ə nəl] **51** 55, **58** 29
terminal building [türm/ ə nəl bĭl/ dĭng] **57** 16
termite [tür/ mīt] **63** 11
terrier [tĕr/ ē ər] **69** 25
test tube [tĕst/ tōob/] **78** 9
Texas [tĕk/ səs] **73** 43
textbook [tĕkst/ bŏok/] **76** 26
theater [thē/ ə tər] **99**
thermometer
   [thər möm/ ə tər] **25** 5, **78** 22
thermos [thür/ məs] **88** 14
thigh [thī] **4** 18, **11** 19
thimble [thĭm/ bəl] **101** 21
third (1/3) [thürd] **79** 32
third baseman [thürd/ bās/ mən] **93** 4
thorn [thörn] **60** 18c
thread [thrĕd] **37** 42b, **101** 2
three-piece suit [thrē/ pēs sōot] **21** 40
throat [thrōt] **5** 59
through [thrōo] **103** 1

throw [thrō] **97** 10
thumb [thŭm] **4** 24
thumbtack [thŭm/ tăk/] **76** 25
ticket [tĭk/ ət] **55** 16, **56** 4
ticket window [tĭk/ ət wĭn/ dō] **55** 19
tie (n) [tī] **21** 47
tie (v) [tī] **77** 12
tie clip [tī/ klĭp/] **23** 14
tie pin [tī/ pĭn/] **23** 13
tiger [tī/ gər] **68** 2
tight [tīt] **24** 3
tighten [tī/ tən] **38** 4
tight end [tīt/ ĕnd/] **93** 30
tights [tīts] **19** 14
tile [tīl] **34** 27
timer [tī/ mər] **78** 13
timetable [tīm/ tă/ bəl] **55** 20
tip [tĭp] **55** 22
tire [tīr] **50** 37, **52** 28
tissues [tĭsh/ ōoz] **32** 13
title [tī/ təl] **47** 9
to [tōo] **103** 9
toast [tōst] **18** 34
toaster [tōs/ tər] **30** 16
toe [tō] **5** 54
toenail [tō/ nāl/] **5** 56
toilet [toy/ lət] **34** 29
toilet brush [toy/ lət brŭsh/] **34** 31
toilet paper [toy/ lət pā/ pər] **34** 30
toiletries [toy/ lə trēz] **23**
token booth [tō/ kən bōoth/] **54** 13
tollbooth [tōl/ bōoth/] **53** 27
tomato(es) [tə mā/ tō(z)] **7** 19
tongs [tŏngz] **78** 29
tongue [tŭng] **4** 41
tongue depressor [tŭng/ də prĕs/ ər] **40** 12a
toolbox [tōol/ bŏks/] **36** 23
toolshed [tōol/ shĕd/] **27** 28
tooth [tōoth] **4** 42
toothache [tōoth/ āk/] **40** 9
toothbrush [tōoth/ brŭsh/] **34** 21
toothless mammals [tōoth/ ləs măm/ əlz] **66**
toothpaste [tōoth/ pāst/] **34** 16
tortoise [tör/ təs] **65** 18
tossed salad [töst/ săl/ əd] **18** 13
touch [tŭch] **77** 2

touring handlebars
[to͞or/ ĭng hăn/ dəl bärz] **52** 12

tow truck [tō/ trŭk] **49** 2

toward [törd] **103** 4

towel rack [tow/ əl răk/] **34** 25

towrope [tō/ rōp/] **59** 11

toy chest [toy/ chĕst/] **33** 29

track [trăk] **54** 10, **94** 32

track and field [trăk/ ənd fēld/] **94**

tractor [trăk/ tər] **81** 15

tractor trailer [trăk/ tər trā/ lər] **49** 15

traffic cop [trăf/ ək kŏp/] **44** 10

traffic light [trăf/ ək līt/] **45** 21

trailer [trā/ lər] **53** 10

train [trān] **55**

training wheels [trān/ ĭng wēlz/] **52** 1

transcript [trăn/ skrĭpt] **43** 15

transfer [trăns/ fər] **54** 4

transformer [trăns för/ mər] **80** 25

transmission towers
[trănz mĭsh/ ən tow/ ərz] **80** 23

transportation [trăns/ pər tā/ shən] **54**

transporter [trăns/ pör tər] **49** 17

trash basket [trăsh/ băs/ kət] **44** 15

trash can [trăsh/ kăn/] **87** 11

travel agent [trăv/ əl ā/ jənt] **84** 4

traveler [trăv/ ə lər] **56** 3

tray [trā] **16** 33

tray table [trā/ tā/ bəl] **56** 22

treatments [trēt/ mənts] **41**

tree [trē] **61** 35

trees [trēz] **60**

triangle [trī/ ăng/ gəl] **79** 6

tricycle [trī/ sĭ kəl] **52** 6

trigger [trĭg/ ər] **48** 22

tripod [trī/ pod] **100** 9

trim [trĭm] **26** 8

trombone [trŏm bōn/] **98** 23

trough [tröf] **81** 25

trout [trowt] **65** 2

trowel [trow/ əl] **27** 27

truck [trŭk] **49, 53** 25

truck driver [trŭk/ drī/ vər] **49** 16

trumpet [trŭm/ pət] **98** 25

trunk [trŭngk] **51** 40, **61** 35b, **66** 17a

tub [tŭb] **12** 6

tuba [to͞o/ bə] **98** 27

tube [to͞ob] **13** 15, **91** 29

tugboat [tŭg/ bōt/] **58** 13

tulip [to͞o/ ləp] **60** 1

turkey [tür/ kē] **10** 23, **64** 20

turnip [tür/ nəp] **7** 34

turn signal lever [türn/ sĭg nəl lĕ/ vər]
50 11

turn signal lights [türn/ sĭg nəl līts/]
51 50

turnstile [türn/ stīl/] **54** 12

turntable [türn/ tā/ bəl] **100** 18

turtle [tür/ təl] **65** 12

(turtleneck) sweater
[tür/ təl nĕk swĕ/ tər] **19** 13

tusk [tŭsk] **66** 17b

TV antenna [tē/ vē ăn tĕn/ ə] **27** 3

tweezers [twē/ zərz] **78** 32

twig [twĭg] **61** 33a

(two-door) sedan [to͞o/ dör sə dăn/] **51**

type [tīp] **77** 10

typewriter [tīp/ rī/ tər] **83** 10

typing chair [tī/ pĭng chër/] **83** 17

typist [tī/ pəst] **83** 6

U.S. mailbox [yo͞o/ ĕs māl/ bŏks] **46** 6

U.S. Postal System
[yo͞o/ ĕs pōs/ təl sĭs təm] **46**

ukulele [yo͞o/ kə lā/ lē] **98** 3

umbrella [ŭm brĕl/ ə] **20** 24

umpire [ŭm/ pīr] **92** 1, **93** 17

uncle [ŭng/ kəl] **3** 3

under [ŭn/ dər] **102** 8

underpants [ŭn/ dər pănts/] **22** 3

undershirt [ŭn/ dər shürt/] **22** 1

underwear [ŭn/ dər wër/] **22**

uniform [yo͞o/ nə förm/] **21** 45, **92** 9

United States of America
[yo͞o nī/ təd stāts/ əv əmër/ ə kə] **72**

universe [yo͞o/ nə vürs/] **74**

up [ŭp] **103** 11

upper arm [ŭp/ ər ärm/] **4** 7

Urals [yo͝or/ əlz] **71** 46

uranium rods [yo͞o rā/ nē əm rŏdz/]
80 15

Uranus [yo͝or/ ə nəs] **74** 17

usher [ŭsh/ ər] **99** 16

Utah [yo͞o/ tö] **73** 44

utility pole [yo͞o tĭl/ ə tē pōl/] **80** 26

utility room [yo͞o tĭl/ ə tē ro͞om] **35**

(V-neck) sweater [vē/ nĕk swĕt/ ər]
19 23

vacuum [văk/ yo͞om] **38** 14

vacuum cleaner [văk/ yo͞om· klē/ nər]
35 16

valve [vălv] **52** 27

van [văn] **53** 26

vase [vās] **28** 6

VCR (videocassette recorder)
[vē/ sē är/ γ
[vĭd/ ē ō kə sĕt/ rə kör/ dər] **100** 4

vegetables [vĕj/ tə bəlz] **6**

vehicles and equipment
[vē/ ə kəlz ənd ə kwĭp/ mənt] **48**

vein [vān] **5** 68

vendor [vĕn/ dər] **87** 3

vent [vĕnt] **50** 21

Venus [vē/ nəs] **74** 12

verbs [vürbz] **17, 26, 31, 38, 77, 96**

Vermont [vür mŏnt/] **73** 45

vest [vĕst] **21** 39

video [vĭd/ē ō] **100**

video camera [vĭd/ ē ō kăm/ ə rə]
100 1

videocassette (tape)
[vĭd/ ē ō kə sĕt/ tāp/] **100** 3

vine [vīn] **61** 42

viola [vē ōl/ ə] **98** 8

violet [vī/ ə lət] **60** 16

violin [vī ə lĭn/] **98** 7

Virginia [vər jĭn/ yə] **73** 46

vise [vīs] **37** 36

visor [vĭz/ ər] **50** 5

volleyball [vŏl/ ē böl/] **92, 92** 22

waders [wā/ dərz] **88** 10

waist [wāst] **4** 13

waiter [wā tər] **16** 5

waitress [wā/ trəs] **16** 2

walk [wök] **77** 8

walker [wök/ ər] **33** 23

wall [wöl] **28** 3

wall unit [wöl/ yo͞o/ nət] **28** 19

wall-to-wall carpeting
[wöl/ tə wöl kär/ pə tĭng] **28** 15

wallet [wöl/ ət] **20** 9

walnut(s) [wöl/ nət(s)] **9** 29

walrus [wöl/ rŭs] **68** 11

warm [wörm] **25** 8

wash [wŏsh] **38** 16
washcloth [wŏsh/klöth/] **34** 22
washer [wŏsh/ər] **37** 40
washing machine
  [wŏsh/ĭng mə shēn/] **35** 30
Washington [wŏsh/ĭng tən] **73** 47
wasp [wŏsp] **63** 20
wastepaper basket
  [wāst/pā pər bǎs/kət] **34** 13
watch [wŏch] **23** 10
watchband [wŏch/bǎnd/] **23** 11
water (n) [wŏt/ər] **42** 16, **91** 30
water (v) [wŏt/ər] **26** 5
water fountain [wŏt/ər fown/tən]
  87 19
water glass [wŏt/ər glǎs/] **29** 6
waterfall [wŏt/ər föl] **80** 11, **89** 18
water-skier [wŏt/ər skē/ər] **59** 10
watercress [wŏt/ər krĕs/] **6** 5
watering can [wŏt/ər ĭng kǎn/] **27** 16
watermelon [wŏt/ər mĕl/ən] **9** 26
wave [wāv] **91** 24
weapon [wĕp/ənz] **48**
weather [wĕdh/ər] **25**
weather forecaster
  [wĕdh/ər för/kǎst ər] **86** 1
weather satellite [wĕdh/ər sǎt/ə līt]
  75 3
weaving [wē/vĭng] **101** 30
web [wĕb] **63** 15
wedding ring [wĕd/ĭng rĭng/] **23** 4
weights [wāts] **78** 5
west [wĕst] **71** 74
West Virginia [wĕst/vər jĭn/yə] **73** 48
wet [wĕt] **25** 15
wet suit [wĕt/sōot/] **91** 38
whale [wāl] **68** 9

wheat [wēt] **60** 22
wheat farm [wēt/färm/] **81**
(wheat) field [wēt/fēld/] **81** 16
wheel [wēl] **52** 4
wheelbarrow [wēl/bǎr/ō] **27** 32,
  82 23
wheelchair [wēl/chër/] **39** 2
whistle [wĭs/əl] **90** 5
whole [hōl] **11** 27, **79** 29
whole (chicken) [hōl/chĭk/ən] **11** 16
width [wĭdth] **79** 35
wife [wīf] **2** 4
willow [wĭl/ō] **61** 31
wind [wĭnd] **80** 4
windbreaker [wĭnd/brā/kər] **19** 5
windlass [wĭnd/ləs] **58** 23
windmill [wĭnd/mĭl/] **80** 19
window [wĭn/dō] **27** 7, **46** 15
window cleaner [wĭn/dō klē/nər]
  35 10
windpipe [wĭnd/pīp/] **5** 60
windshield [wĭnd/shēld/] **51** 45
windshield wiper [wĭnd/shēld wī/pər]
  50 6
windsurfer [wĭnd/sür/fər] **59** 14
windy [wĭn/dē] **25** 13
wine [wīn] **16** 19
wine glass [wīn/glǎs/] **29** 5
wing [wĭng] **11** 22, **57** 9, **63** 4a,
  64 1a
Winter [wĭn/tər] **26**
wipe [wīp] **38** 5
wire [wīr] **37** 35
wire mesh screen [wīr/mĕsh skrēn/]
  78 6
Wisconsin [wĭs kŏn/sən] **73** 49
witness [wĭt/nəs] **43** 13

witness stand [wĭt/nəs stǎnd/] **43** 18
wolf [wŏolf] **69** 29
woman [wŏom/ən] **2** 1
wood [wŏod] **36** 4
wood plane [wŏod/plān/] **37** 32
woodpecker [wŏod/pĕk/ər] **64** 17
woods [wŏodz] **89** 32
woodwinds [wŏod/wĭndz/] **98**
wool [wŏol] **101** 23
word processor [würd/prŏ/sĕs ər]
  83 7
work gloves [würk/glŭvz/] **27** 26
workbench [würk/bĕnch/] **36** 22
workshop [würk/shŏp/] **36**
world [würld]
worm [würm] **62** 11
wrench [rĕnch] **36** 10
wrist [rĭst] **4** 21
write [rīt] **77** 7
writer [rī/tər] **86** 7
Wyoming [wī ō/mĭng] **73** 50
X ray [ĕks/rā/] **39** 1
X ray screener [ĕks/rā skrē/nər] **56** 11
xylophone [zī/lə fōn/] **98** 31
yam [yǎm] **7** 24
Yangtze River [yǎng/sē rĭv/ər] **71** 69
yarn [yärn] **101** 31
Yellow Sea [yĕl/ō sē/] **70** 37
Yenisey River [yĕn/ə sā/rĭv/ər]
  71 65
Yukon River [yōo/kŏn rĭv/ər] **71** 56
zebra [zē/brə] **66** 18
zinnia [zĭn/ē ə] **60** 13
zip code [zĭp/kōd/] **46** 12
zipper [zĭp/ər] **101** 16
zoo [zōo] **87** 1
zucchini [zōo kē/nē] **7** 27